PLANTS & GARDENS

BROOKLYN BOTANIC GARDEN RECORD

GARDENING WITH WILDFLOWERS & NATIVE PLANTS

1990

Brooklyn Botanic Garden

STAFF FOR THE ORIGINAL EDITION:

CLAIRE E. SAWYERS, GUEST EDITOR

BARBARA B. PESCH, EDITOR

JO KEIM, ASSOCIATE EDITOR

STAFF FOR THE REVISED EDITION:

BARBARA B. PESCH, DIRECTOR OF PUBLICATIONS

JANET MARINELLI, ASSOCIATE EDITOR

AND THE EDITORIAL COMMITTEE OF THE BROOKLYN BOTANIC GARDEN

BEKKA LINDSTROM, ART DIRECTOR

DONALD E. MOORE, PRESIDENT, BROOKLYN BOTANIC GARDEN

ELIZABETH SCHOLTZ, VICE PRESIDENT, BROOKLYN BOTANIC GARDEN

COVER PHOTO: MT. CUBA CENTER, BY CLAIRE SAWYERS
ALL PHOTOGRAPHS BY CLAIRE E. SAWYERS EXCEPT WHERE NOTED

Plants and Gardens, Brooklyn Botanic Garden Record (ISSN 0362-5850) is published quarterly at 1000 Washington Ave., Brooklyn, N.Y. 11225, by the **Brooklyn Botanic Garden, Inc.** Second-class-postage paid at Brooklyn, N.Y., and at additional mailing offices. Subscription included in Botanic Garden membership dues ($20.00) per year.
Copyright © 1989, 1990 by the Brooklyn Botanic Garden, Inc.

GARDENING WITH WILDFLOWERS & NATIVE PLANTS

THIS HANDBOOK IS A REVISED EDITION OF PLANTS & GARDENS, VOL. 45, NO. 1

A naturalistic setting at the Mt. Cuba Center in Greenville, Delaware.

NOTE FROM THE GUEST EDITOR

There are a few things you should know before you start reading the wealth of information about American native plants found between these covers. First, the basic reference used for scientific names is *A Synonymized Checklist of the Vascular Flora of the United States, Canada and Greenland.* Produced by John and Rosemarie Kartesz, it was published in 1980 by the University of North Carolina Press. Dr. Ritchie Bell, who has contributed to this handbook, assisted with the checklist. It is the most recent and comprehensive accounting of North American plant species.

Second, some of the plant combinations offered in the articles here include exotic plants. Throughout the handbook, an exotic is defined as any plant not native to the U.S., and is identified by an asterisk (*) following its name.

Third, the hardiness zones referred to throughout the handbook are those of the USDA Plant Hardiness Zone Map, as shown on page 91.

One other thing I'd like to add: In 1851, Andrew Jackson Downing wrote:

Nothing strikes foreign horticulturists and amateurs so much as this apathy and indifference of Americans to the beautiful sylvan and floral products of their own country. An enthusiastic collector in Belgium first made us keenly sensible of this condition of our countrymen, last summer, in describing the difficulty he had in procuring from any of his correspondents here, American seeds or plants, even of well known and tolerably abundant species, by telling us that amateurs and nurserymen who annually import from him every new and rare exotic that the richest collections of Europe possessed, could scarcely be prevailed upon to make a search for native American plants, far more beautiful, which grow in the woods not ten miles from their own doors. Some of them were wholly ignorant of such plants, except so far as a familiarity with their names in the books may be called and acquaintance. Others knew them, but considered them 'wild plants,' and therefore, too little deserving of attention to be worth the trouble of collecting, even for curious foreigners. 'And so,' he continued 'in a country of azaleas, kalmias, rhododendrons, cypripediums, magnolias and nyssas—the loveliest flowers, shrubs, and trees of temperate climates—you never put them in your gardens, but send over the water every year for thousands of dollars worth of English larches and Dutch hyacinths. Voilà le goût Republicain!'

Sadly, while Downing was tremendously influential regarding garden design, this quote could have been written yesterday (except perhaps for the dated writing style). It is my hope that the contributors who wrote passionately for this handbook will inspire you to plant some of "the loveliest flowers, shrubs and trees of temperate climates" in your garden.

* Quoted from *Rural Essays* first written for the *Horticulturist* and later collected by George William Curtis and published in book form in 1851.

CLAIRE SAWYERS *is administrative assistant/acting curator at Mt. Cuba Center in Greenville, DE, where she has learned much about native plants. She is free-lance garden writer and a regional director of the Garden Writers of America Association (1989-1991). She holds masters degrees in plant science from Purdue University and the University of Delaware. She was guest editor of* **Plants & Gardens** *handbooks* **Japanese Gardens** *(1985) and* **American Gardens: A Traveler's Guide** *(1986).*

ILLUSTRATION BY NETTIE S. SMITH

WHY NATIVE PLANTS

HARRISON L. FLINT

*The following address was made at
the 1986 Longwood Graduate
Program Seminar.*

Before considering why we should use native plants in landscaping, we need to consider the more important question: Why should we preserve native plants?

Reasons for preserving native plants fall into two general categories:

ECOLOGICAL REASONS have to do with how plants function in ecosystems. Extinction, the ultimate catastrophe for a species, is a one-way passage. Species are products of thousands or even millions of years of evolution. Once they are lost, replacement is so slow that, in the human time scale, it does not happen. There are other catastrophes as well. Ecosystems depend not just on the survival of a few remaining individuals, but on adequate numbers for interaction within the ecosystem. Rarely if ever do we know what population level is necessary, but our knowledge of ecosystems tells us there must be a level

for each species. Moreover, survival of a species, especially in capricious climates, depends on maintaining a broad level of variation in the gene pool. So the population of a rare species in more important not just for the functioning of the ecosystem, but for the survival of the species itself.

HUMAN REASONS, Homo sapiens, the species we belong to, is a strange member of our ecosystem, although we may not acknowledge or even recognize the fact. Our dependence on plant species for food, shelter and medicine is well known. We are also gripped by a psychic dependence on plants which make our surroundings familiar to us. In doing so, they give us a sense of protection, comfort, peace, and even inspiration. In the richness of their diversity they contribute to our human delight.

There are many different ways to use native plants. The most complex way is to reconstruct a plant community, or a significant part of one. The least complex is merely an "affirmative action" program to include more of the best native plants in nursery lists and in the palettes of landscape designers.

Efforts to promote the use of native plants have been going on for a long time

HARRISON L. FLINT *has taught at Purdue University in the area of woody landscape plants since 1968. At Purdue, he initiated the Professional Plantsman Program for students pursuing careers in botanical gardens and related institutions. Professor Flint has authored many popular and scientific articles and two books.* **Landscape Plants for Eastern North America** *has received two national awards. His* **The Country Journal Book of Hardy Trees and Shrubs** *describes landscape plants for cold climates.*

Close-up view of the flowers of *Fothergilla major*. The flower clusters are upright, with a bottlebrush shape. They appear as the leaves are unfolding.

in the Midwest, with the activities of pioneers like O.C. Simonds, who is often though of as the father of the movement, and Jens Jensen, no purist in the use of native plants, yet a tremendous influence through his sensitive creation of landscapes that emulate nature. Another pioneer was the great communicator, May Theilgaard Watts. Her lifetime of teaching and writing about nature and natural landscapes at the Morton Arboretum, well sampled in her book, *Reading The Landscape*, educated several generations and set the stage for Ray Schulenberg's work in prairie restoration at the same institution.

Restoring Native Plant Communities

The complexity of most ecosystems, with their full range of plants, animals and micro-flora, makes full restoration practically impossible. The most ambitious efforts to date have included partly reconstructed communities of plants and animals. More often, restoration of native landscapes has been limited to most or part of the higher plant complement — overstory and understory trees, shrubs, and ground covers. Interest in this approach is increasing, and a growing number of landscape architects in this country and others are now devoting much of their time to constructing landscapes with native communities.

According to practitioners, reconstructed native plant communities offer specific advantages:

REGIONAL UNIQUENESS. Native plant communities preserve in a region a *genius loci*, or pervading spirit that makes each place unique, identifiable, familiar and comfortable to its residents. When finished, a constructed landscape that emulates nature may once again express those qualities which first attracted us to the natural landscape.

INTEGRITY. With nature as inspiration, native plant communities give a feeling of wholeness and inherent compatibility. Such landscapes are in tune with seasonal changes of land and climate, and express this visually by their own seasonal changes. They serve as extensions of the greater landscape.

EDUCATIONAL AND RECREATIONAL VALUE. Living within a native plant community offers endless opportunities for observation of nature, with its attendant educational and recreational benefits. Our psychic roots draw us to nature, even when we resist. We sense that interaction with plant life can greatly ameliorate stress.

Using Native Plants in Mixed Landscapes

Native plant communities are useful in many types of landscapes, including urban sites. Yet in some situations their use is difficult or even impossible. Even when native communities cannot be reintroduced, native species are still useful. Their best use in such situations may be in artificial but visually compatible groupings, combined with non-native species that are fitted to the site because of adaptation to similar conditions in other parts of the world where they have evolved.

In mixed (native and non-native) landscapes, we attempt to imitate or even step beyond nature's exemplary combining of plant species. In selecting plant combinations, we set out to achieve in a mortal life span what has taken nature thousands of years to accomplish. If we recognize that we are doing this, we may assume an attitude of humility that will allow us to create landscapes, yet maintain a proper sense of generosity toward nature. It seems ethically essential that we give our first attention to nature itself, by conserving natural ecosystems, before turning to our constructed gardens and landscapes. This is a lesson we largely have yet to learn but I think we are making progress. 🌺

SNOWBERRY
(Symphoricarpos)

THE SOURCE OF OUR WILDFLOWERS

THE MODERN FLORA OF NORTH AMERICA

C. RITCHIE BELL

W hen we garden with native and naturalized wildflowers, we garden not only with nature but also with history. Since many of our showy wildflowers have been of medicinal, economic or other importance in earlier cultures, the historical aspect often adds further insight and enjoyment to our gardening efforts.

Many of the *native* plants among the wildflowers in our gardens today are a part of the vast array of strange, useful and beautiful plants of the "new world" that provided the early European explorers and settlers with the food, fuel, shelter and medicines necessary for survival. Other wildflowers we grow may actually be colorful plants from other lands that have been introduced into America and naturalized

C. RICHIE BELL, *professor of botany and, for 25 years (1960-1985), director of the North Carolina Botanical Garden, is active in public education and conservation concerning our native plants. He wrote North Carolina's current plant protection law; and was co-author of the **Manual of the Vascular Flora of the Carolinas** and two popular books: **Wild Flowers of North Carolina** and **Florida Wild Flowers and Roadside Plants**. He received the 1979 National Council of Garden Clubs Silver Seal Award for work in conservation.*

— that is, they grow wild, they thrive and spread without human help. A current printout from the extensive computerized Kartesz database for North American plants at the North Carolina Botanical Garden shows almost 3,000 species, or about 16% of our total flora of some 18,000 species, to be introduced. Perhaps, when our records are complete, we will find that about half of these introduced plants are now truly naturalized while others may only be waifs or rare escapes from cultivation that do not survive without human care.

Some of our naturalized plants are so prolific and so adaptable biologically that, despite their interest, beauty or fragrance, they are often considered to be weeds! The dandelion (*Taraxacum officinale*, from Europe), Queen Anne's Lace (*Daucus carota*, from the Afghanistan area by way of Europe) and Japanese honeysuckle (*Lonicera japonica*, from Japan) are good examples of introduced plants that have become weedy. However, even though considered weeds in many situations, these plants may still have a valid place in a wildflower garden if they are appropriately confined.

Mt. Rainer provides a panoramic backdrop for a field of lupines in the foreground. Native species will do best in the garden with conditions similar to their native habitat.

Maine's Isle-aux-Haut has its own unique set of environmental factors that play an essential part in the forming plant communities found there.

Not all weeds, however, are introduced plants. With the clearing of the forests over the past three centuries and the disruption of the stable, mature or climax plant communities, quite a few native American plants, such as the blackberries (*Rubus* spp.), poison oak and ivy (*Toxicodendron* spp.), wild onions (*Allium* spp.) and even cattails (*Typha* spp.) have spread rapidly and become terrestrial or aquatic weeds in many areas. Indeed, if we define a weed as "any plant growing out of place"

West Virginia's forests are mixed Southeastern forests.
In many areas where logging has cleared the land second- and
third-growth pines have replaced the hardwoods.

we can see why some attractive but prolific native plants, such as the rhizomatous wild ginger (*Asarum canadense*) or the common blue violet (*Viola priceana*), or even the beautiful New England aster (*Aster novae-angliae*) and cardinal flower (*Lobelia cardinalis*) can, without some control, become a weed in our wildflower garden. Thus the term "weed" and "wildflower" can only be defined in specific contexts and through the eyes of the beholder. For example: little bellwort (*Uvularia sessilifolia*), a delicate spring ephemeral of the southern Appalachians, is often listed as a desirable perennial for the wildflower garden and, oddly, it is also listed as a weed by the Weed Science Society of America. Indeed, among the nearly 2,000 plants on this subjective and unofficial list, one finds a number of showy natives (the bladderworts, *Utricularia* spp. for instance) that are also on one or more of the various state lists of "rare and endangered" native plants. So don't fear having a few attractive "weeds" in your wildflower garden!

The great diversity of plant life in North America was a source of amazement to early explorers and, of course, reflected the great diversity of climates, soils and local environments within this vast area. Every new range of mountains, every new river valley, and each new strip of coastal dunes or swampland provided new plants of such interest, beauty or utility that fine timber, drugs and plants of horticultural value soon made up many of the cargoes bound for Europe from the Colonies. As these plants from America became established in the gardens of Europe, they confirmed the seemingly outlandish reports of the early explorers who told of huge *evergreen* trees (*Magnolia!*) with fragrant flowers nearly a foot across, or of plants with hollow leaves (*Sarracenia*) that trapped insects, or even of a plant (*Dionaea*) with leaves that moved to trap insects!

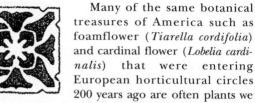

Many of the same botanical treasures of America such as foamflower (*Tiarella cordifolia*) and cardinal flower (*Lobelia cardinalis*) that were entering European horticultural circles 200 years ago are often plants we find to be attractive subjects for our wildflower gardens today. However, we must be realistic in our selections from the much larger number of native species now known and available to gardeners. We must keep in mind that certain groups of tree, shrub and herb species are adapted to grow together as a "plant community" under a particular set of environmental conditions (temperature, light, soil, moisture) and will do best in your garden if provided with conditions similar to those of their native habitat.

Most gardeners are familiar with the 10 minimum temperature zones of North America, reproduced in many seed catalogs as the "plant hardiness zone" map (see p. 91 herein), which shows a minimum temperature range from the -40 degrees to -30 degrees F of the sometimes frigid Zone 3 to the usually subtropical 30 degrees to 40 degrees F minimum of Zone 10. These 10 temperature or "climatic zones" overlay a mosaic of a dozen or more different kinds of soil (sand, clay, loam, etc.) which, in turn, may have different altitudes, slopes, acidity or water-holding capacity. As a result of the various combinations of environmental factors we find a corresponding variation in the plant communities. Thus over 100 specialized plant communities, each generally named for the dominant cover plant or plants in the association, have been recognized for North America. The plants of each of these communities are adapted to a specific major climate/soil combination and some of these major plant communities cover, or originally covered, thousands of square miles. Today, however, urban growth, road and highway, construction, our agricultural needs, and our need for paper, timber and other forest products have reduced many of these once vast dominant-plant communities to small remnants tucked away here and there protected by concerned groups and individuals as reserves or special conservation areas.

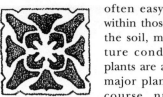

Along the East Coast the major plant communities are forests such as the evergreen Spruce-Fir Community of high altitudes and latitudes, with the Beech-Maple, Mixed Mesophytic and Pine-Oak-Hickory Communities at the lower altitudes and latitudes. However, in many areas second- and third-growth pines have replaced the hardwoods as they have been logged. Some of the smaller, more specialized and often more botanically unique plant communities of the Northeast are such associations as the Pine Barrens of New Jersey, the Cedar Glades of Tennessee, Missouri and Alabama, the Southern Coastal Plain Pocosins, the Southern Cordgrass Prairie and, of course, the Everglades of southern Florida.

In the Great Central Plains, some of the important original grassland associations were: the Bluestem Prairie, Grama-Buffalo Grass and Bluestem-Grama Prairie. Further west we find major areas of the Great Basin Sagebrush Community, Creosote Bush, Mesquite-Acacia Savanna, Palo Verde-Cactus Shrub, and Chaparral Community. Along the West Coast itself some of the major plant communities, again often found now only as protected remnants of once widespread plant-covers types, are the Redwood Forest, Douglas Fir Forest, Juniper-Pinon Woodland, Oak-Juniper Woodland, Coastal Sagebrush, and of course, the grasslands or California Steppe.

Each of the above major plant communities has its own distinctive group of colorful, interesting, annual and perennial herbaceous plants which make excellent choices for wildflower gardens and are often easy to grow in gardens within those regions that provide the soil, moisture and temperature conditions to which the plants are adapted. Within each major plant community are, of course, numerous small and more specialized plant populations and communities specifically adapted to, and often limited to, a relatively infrequent combination of very specific soil, moisture, light and temperature factors. Some of these highly specialized plant communities may be defined primarily by specific soil factors; for example, the Shale Barrens and Diabase Dike communities of the East or the Serpentine communities of the West. Others, such as the plant communities found on the shallow soil of granite outcrops, are adapted to highly acidic pools, seasonally available, on these bare-rock surfaces. Plants of the famous cranberry bogs of the Northeast also thrive in highly acidic, but almost constantly wet, conditions of the sphagnum/peat substrate.

Many beautiful wildflowers of the more highly specialized plant communities are so strongly adapted to the special conditions of these communities that they are found nowhere else. Such plants of specific, usually restricted, habitat and range are referred to as "endemic" plants and, because of their restricted range and generally small population size, may be quite rare. Fortunately, more and more of these rare endemics, determined by botanists to be endangered, are being given legal protection by the Federal and state governments to help save them from extinction by overzealous plant collectors, uncontrolled commercial exploitation, or the thoughtless destruction of their specialized habitats. However, these highly specialized plant communities can still provide many other beautiful wildflowers for those gardens where the specific habitat requirements for such species can be rather closely duplicated.

This prairie at the Shaw Arboretum in St. Louis, Missouri features the native coneflower, *Echinacea purpurea*.

Among our endangered endemics (and the "difficult or impossible to grow" wildflowers) are many species which have, in addition to very specific soil, climate and light requirements for growth, a very complex nutritional association with specific fungi that live in the roots of the plants and actually provide some (or all!) of the food or certain raw materials needed by the host plant to grow, flower and set seed. In many cases, we do not even know the name of the fungus in these intricate symbiotic relationships, let alone what *its* environmental requirements are — and, if the fungus dies, its host dies. This is why the "mycorrhizal plants", such as Indian pipe (*Monotropa*

flower garden. On the other hand, some of our showy and interesting parasitic wildflowers such as Indian paintbrush (*Castilleja* spp.) which is parasitic on the roots of grasses and some shrubs, false foxglove (*Aureolaria*, spp.) parasitic on the roots of oaks and beechdrops (*Epifagus virginiana*), parasitic on the roots of beech can often be grown from seed if you have the appropriate host plant in your garden.

To have a more beautiful, healthy and carefree wildflower garden, learn the lesson of our plant communities. If you live on the seacoast, you should certainly plan a garden of native and naturalized coastal wildflowers (but remember that the plants of the eastern and western seacoasts are certainly quite different!); if you live in the mountains (eastern or western, see above!), put mountain plants in your garden. If, within a given region, your garden has some special environmental condition such as a moist area, a shady area, an open area or specialized soil type, you can almost guarantee success with your wildflower garden by planting each "habitat" with those trees, shrubs or herbs of your region that are naturally adapted to your particular combination of conditions.

Generally, the more widespread a particular plant species, the more generalized are its environmental requirements and the easier it will be to raise in your garden. Conversely, the more geographically or ecologically restricted a plant species, the more specialized and specific are its environmental requirements and the more difficult it may be to grow under other soil, moisture, light or nutritional conditions. Of course, the greater the challenge such plants offer the grower, the greater the satisfaction in growing them and the more valuable the propagation and cultural information derived from the gardener's records of successes and failures in propagation and establishment of such "difficult" plants in their gardens. 🌱

uniflora), pine-sap (*Monotropa hypopithys*) and snow plant (*Sarcodes sanguinea*) in the Monotropaceae, or Indian Pipe Family; small whorled pogonia (*Isotria medeoloides*), the lady-slippers (*Cypripedium* spp.) and most other members of the Orchidaceae, or Orchid Family, cannot be transplanted and should not be attempted in the wild-

ACQUIRING NATIVE PLANTS

MARY POCKMAN

I n choosing plants, gardeners who cherish the plants of wild places add another criterion to the usual emphasis on quality: conservation. We seek to acquire the best garden plants, and to acquire them in ways that respect the integrity of natural communities, in all their beauty and diversity.

The criterion of quality is familiar to all gardeners. Peonies or penstemons, Kurume azaleas or mountain laurels, the plants of choice are always those that in appearance and vigor will add most to the place and special mood that the gardener envisions. By this standard, the plants to select are those intentionally propagated for garden use, something that hardly needs to be said about familiar cultivated plants.

When it comes to wildflowers and other native species, however, intentional propagation cannot be taken for granted. Many if not most of the plants now available have been removed from their wild habitats. Plants dug from the wild are generally much less satisfactory in the garden. Moreover, wild collection for garden use is a

MARY POCKMAN, *a conservationist and longtime wildflower enthusiast with a weakness for ferns, is past president (1985-1988) of the Virginia Native Plant Society. She began using native species in her own garden in northwest Connecticut in the 1960s. In her present garden, in suburban Washington, D.C., she grows some 70 native species.*

dubious practice in terms of conservation. Many native species are already under severe pressure because of shrinking natural habitats and a compromised environment.

To avoid jeopardizing wild populations and yet obtain the highest quality plants, it is best to search out propagated plants and decline those dug from the wild — with the exception of plants removed from sites where they would otherwise be obliterated. Putting this policy into practice is not difficult, but it does require attention and care.

The advantages of propagated plants are clear cut. Unlike plants that have come to maturity in the wild, they have been grown under favorable conditions and protected against serious pests, competition and undue stress. They are thus generally healthier and better looking, with more compact and vigorous root systems. Wild-collected plants often disappoint gardeners by sulking or disappearing completely; propagated plants far more consistently live up to expectations.

The argument against wild collection on grounds of conservation is more complex. Horticultural collection is extensive, and it is potentially harmful; that much is clear. There is little systematic information, however, about its extent, or, more important, its impact. (Much, or even most, wild collection is believed to be illegal, violating laws regarding theft, trespass or taking

ILLUSTRATION BY NETTIE S. SMITH

from public lands; this could in part explain the lack of data.) More-over, there is constant change in the practice of wild collection itself, in its environmental context, and in perceptions of its risks.

Not too long ago, digging garden plants from the wild was the usual practice, rarely questioned. A few enthusiasts grew their own, but nurseries and horticulturists for the most part ignored native species. In the eyes of most people, America's vast uncultivated lands and their plants were a limitless resource.

As wild lands have been steadily converted to human use and the shadow of environmental problems has spread, that blithe optimism has waned. In its place is growing appreciation for the value and the vulnerability of the natural world, and mounting opposition to practices that may threaten it. Especially as the surge of interest in native plant gardening has pushed demand for plants to new highs, wild collection for garden use has come under increasing criticism.

To the native flora as a whole, horticultural collection is a far less serious threat than habitat loss or such far-reaching changes as deteriorating air and water quality. It can add to other stresses, however, by reducing the size and genetic variability of local populations, disrupting complex ecological relationships, and physically damaging habitats. For species and plant communities already hard-pressed, continued wild collection has the potential to do significant harm.

The commercial trade in collected plants is estimated to involve hundreds of species sold by a profusion of dealers, from nurseries to hardware stores. Sales of a popular species may well total several hundred thousand plants a year. One Federal investigation, for example, documented a year's shipments of more than 75,000 wild-dug orchids by one dealer alone. To plants collected for sale must be added those dug by individuals for their own use.

What's known about the harm done by wild collection is patchy. Horticultural collection is cited as a major factor in the decline of some species, such as the white fringeless orchid, *Platanthera integrilabia*, listed as endangered in Tennessee, and it has virtually eradicated some readily accessible populations of others. Some species are of concern simply because the demand, and thus the number of plants collected, is so great. Others are considered vulnerable because of intrinsic characteristics such as rarity, slow natural reproduction, limited adaptability, or occurrence in fragile habitats. Most at risk may be species that are both much in demand and inherently vulnerable, such as some alpines and cacti or certain lady's-slippers.

Conservationists generally conclude that the risks of horticultural collection are

19

unacceptable, particularly since any harm that results may be irreparable. Given the extent of commercial collection, it may be tempting to rationalize that the number of wild-dug plants one gardener could possibly use makes little difference. It's never just one gardener, however. The cumulative power of many trowels is considerable, and individual purchases of wild-dug plants add up to the demand that perpetuates wild collection.

At the same time wild collection is falling from favor, nursery-propagated plants are becoming much more widely available. Spurred by the popularity of native species, propagators have made substantial advances in finding ways to handle them, including micro-propagation, and this progress is continuing. New nurseries propagating everything they sell have come into the wildflower trade, and established nurseries are propagating more species as effective methods make propagation more profitable than buying from diggers.

Selective breeding of native species is also adding to the availability of propagated plants. Like such garden staples as bearded iris and hybrid daylilies, the resulting selections and cultivars are available only through propagation. The increase in their number, and the expanding use of American natives in formal as well as naturalistic settings, are together blurring the distinction between traditional gardening and wildflower gardening, not only in style but in the origin of plants.

The overall effect of these changes is a gradual shift away from wild collection toward propagation of wildflowers and other native species. It is far from com-

Propagated plants are generally healthier and better looking with more compact and vigorous root systems than wild-collected ones. Nursery-propagated plants are becoming more readily available

plete, however. Long-standing attitudes and practices are slow to change. In addition, growers do not yet know how to propagate some of the most coveted species, and production of others is still too difficult or slow to appear profitable.

During this period of transition, conservation-conscious gardeners need to begin the search for plants with some knowledge about the species that attract them, in particular their propagation and cultivation requirements. Those who choose to buy plants must also look critically at possible sources, recognizing the realities of growing and selling plants as a business.

The simplest strategy is to plan a garden that uses only species that can readily be propagated—not a severe limitation—and to acquire plants either by growing them at home or by buying from nurseries that propagate all their stock. Gardeners able to devote more time and energy to obtaining plants can expand their choices through plant rescues, propagation of more exacting species, and careful checking of other sources.

Given constant change in propagation techniques and nursery practices, any guide to acquiring plants is necessarily general. Up-to-date information is available from a number of publications and organizations (see source lists, p.92); what follows is intended to help put it to work.

A rewarding way to make sure where plants originate is to take charge of the process personally. One time-honored source, a friend's garden, is as appropriate for wildflowers as for other plants. Many species are easy for home gardeners to propagate, including some for which nursery production is not yet feasible. A number of publications give excellent advice on propagation methods, and on obtaining seed, spores or cuttings without reducing the reproductive capacity of wild populations.

Relocating plants that otherwise face certain destruction can provide mature specimens. To improve the chances that rescued or salvaged plants will thrive, minimize the stress of transplanting and give them extra attention.

Plant rescues should have the permission of the landowner, and no plants should be removed from parts of a site that will remain undisturbed. While it's possible for individuals to rescue plants on their own, landowners are more likely to give permission and detailed information to an organized group, such as a garden club or native plant society, especially when a large tract is involved. (For more detailed suggestions on organizing a plant rescue, see Harry R. Phillips, *Growing and Propagating Wild Flowers*, 1985, Chapel Hill: University of North Carolina Press.)

Buying plants is more complicated. Whether plants for sale are nursery propagated or wild collected is sometimes almost impossible to know for certain. The mix of wild-collected and nursery-propagated plants on the market varies widely from one species to another, and few retailers state the origin of the plants they offer. The greater the probable risk of wild collection to the species, the greater the caution that should be exercised in buying plants.

The most straightforward purchases are of plants that for all practical purposes cannot be wild collected—selections and cultivars, as well as at least one species, *Franklinia alatamaha*, that has been extirpated in the wild. Many, such as *Monarda didyma* 'Cambridge Scarlet', are well established in the trade and widely available; those more recently introduced, such as *Kalmia latifolia* 'Olympic Fire', may be harder to find. Some are naturally occurring but uncommon variations, including double forms such as *Sanguinaria canadensis* 'Multiplex' and albinos such as *Lobelia cardinalis* 'Alba'. While an occasional plant could be collected, to dig such forms in quantity would be virtually impossible.

At the other end of the spectrum are species that are virtually always wild collected. Some appeal to too few gardeners to make commercial propagation worthwhile, even though it may not be difficult. More prominent are much-wanted species that so far cannot be propagated or grown on a commercial scale, notably the native orchids, most of which present formidable problems in both propagation and cultivation. Until nursery production of these species becomes feasible, the best choice is to forego buying them; enjoy them in the wild and watch for opportunities to rescue plants.

Between these extremes lies a large and sometimes bewildering group of species that can be and are propagated, but are also collected. Whether one or the other is the more common practice depends on a number of factors, mostly related to the economics of the nursery business. Many are hard for customers to assess.

As a general rule, species that are tricky to propagate or slow to reach marketable size, and thus expensive to produce, are more apt to be wild collected; trilliums, which commonly take five years or more from seed to flower, are one example. Those that are easy to propagate and quick to mature, such as cardinal flower and columbines, are more likely to be nursery propagated. The cost and availability of wild-dug plants must also be considered, however, and many factors besides production cost enter the equation. In any case these are only probabilities, not much help in a particular situation.

Price, by the way, is not a reliable guide. Propagation may be more expensive than wild collection, but expensive plants are not necessarily nursery propagated. Large plants of a slow-growing species, for instance, are generally expensive, and they are very apt to be wild collected.

Some understanding of this background is helpful, but in buying plants of species in this confusing group, a critical look at particular sources is indispensable.

Easiest to start with are those that state explicitly that all the plants they sell are nursery propagated; some add that they do not sell wild-collected plants, and explain why. (What they say isn't necessarily true, of course, it's prudent to test it against what they sell. Would-be deceivers seem more apt just to dodge the issue, though.)

Among this group are some nonprofit organizations committed to native plant conservation. Native plant societies and botanical gardens with a special interest in natives, for example, quite commonly combine public education and fund raising in sales of plants they have propagated.

A small but growing number of commercial nurseries, including many that accept mail orders, also make a point of telling customers that all their wildflowers and native plants are nursery propagated. Although a few are large, general nurseries, most are relatively small. Many of the latter grow all the plants they sell, and their lists often include species that are relatively unfamiliar, or that volume nurseries consider unprofitable to propagate.

The great majority of nurseries, mail-order dealers, and garden centers say nothing about how they acquire plants. No particular meaning should be read into their silence; it's customary for those who sell plants to focus on descriptions and cultural requirements. Don't be misled, however, by phrases that convey no information about the *origin* of the plants, such as "nursery grown" or "field grown, "specially selected" or "bred for garden success." Note other characteristics as well; a feverish sales pitch, careless nomenclature, sketchy cultural information may suggest more serious interest in profits than in plants.

The words to look for are *nursery propagated.* In the absence of that phrase or an unambiguous equivalent, ask about the origin of the plants. Those who know their plants are nursery propagated will say so without hesitation. Nonanswers or evasions, however graceful, should at least trigger further questions, and in some instances send you to another source.

One frequent reply is that plants come from wholesalers. Most local garden centers and probably a majority of mail-order retailers do buy from other nurseries, but they should know or be able to find out how their suppliers obtain plants.

Two common replies may leave unanswerable questions. One is that the plants have been rescued. Some people familiar with the trade maintain that most wild collection is from sites where destruction is imminent, but they also acknowledge that some plants labeled "rescued" have been dug from sites where there is no prospect of disturbance. When the claim of rescue is valid, it does answer objections to wild collection on conservation grounds. Without personal knowledge of the seller and the rescue site, however, its legitimacy is almost impossible to determine.

The second is that plants have been harvested from wild populations on a sustained-yield basis. That is theoretically possible, at least for common, abundant species, although lack of information about population dynamics in a changing environment may make it difficult to determine what yield is sustainable. Like the claim of rescue, however, the claim of carefully gauged harvest is extremely hard to verify. The likelihood that rescued or harvested plants will succeed in the garden is the same as for any wild-collected plants.

As a cross check on the answers a source has given, or when those answers are ambiguous, examination of the plants themselves may give clues to their history. If possible, look at several plants of a species, not just one. Does it seem more likely that they were dug from their wild habitat, or reared from the beginning under nursery conditions? This approach is useful in a local garden center, where it may be difficult to get questions answered, but it can also be instructive as an after-the-fact assessment of plants bought by mail.

Look at the plants' general health. Poor color, sparse foliage, weak stems, legginess, old wounds, all suggest wild collection, not to mention what they say about quality.

Check the size or apparent age, keeping in mind the investment a nursery must make to produce a large plant. Especially in species that grow slowly, large, or obviously older plants, are more likely to be wild collected—for example, ferns with rootstocks carrying the remains of many fronds. On shrubs such as mountain laurel, watch for good-sized stumps near ground level, typical of a wild-dug shrub that has been cut back to stimulate new growth.

Look at the way the plant is potted. Nursery-propagated plants are usually more or less centered in the pot, and their foliage falls naturally.

Are other plants sharing the pot or the root ball? Fast-growing extras may crop up in the tidiest nurseries, but few intentionally propagate mixed clumps. Bonus plants that are also salable—a garland of ferns at the base of a rhododendron, for example, or a Jack-in-the-pulpit in a clump of foamflower—suggest wild collection.

Turn the plant out of its container if possible. Nursery-propagated plants are usually grown in a light, uniform mix, often containing shredded bark or obviously artificial materials such as perlite. Compacted clay, large stones, or different soils in one pot are more likely with wild-collected plants. Allowing for the habits of different species, the root system of a nursery-propagated plant will be relatively compact; it is unlikely to be lopsided, thin and straggly, or patently crammed into the container.

It seems likely that wild collection will eventually be replaced by propagation, but "eventually" may be some time in coming. In the meantime, through care in acquiring plants, gardeners can both add to their own pleasure and take their stand with all who are working to ensure that wildflowers and native plants remain part of a treasured living heritage. 🌿

A clump of pearly everlasting, *Anaphalis margaritacea*, thrives near the tree line at Mount Hood in Oregon.

CREATING A NATURALISTIC GARDEN

Darrel G. Morrison

You don't create a natural-looking garden by simply "letting things go." As appealing as that concept might be from the standpoint of time and energy, there have been too many environmental changes on most residential sites to make that a realistic option. For example, much of the native vegetation has been removed and replaced with imported plants. Hence, a *laissez-faire* approach under such conditions is likely to produce a chaotic mix of native and exotic plants. The process of recreating a natural landscape, or even a natural looking garden requires conscious manipulation and "design."

How do you go about designing "naturalistic" gardens? As a landscape architect convinced of the value of natural appearing landscapes, and as a teacher, I would like to share observations that I have made during the past couple of decades of working with both natural and designed landscapes.

First of all, we can't design gardens that will equal the order, complexity, integrity and beauty of the typical undisturbed natural landscape. But we can learn about design from the processes and forms that occur in such natural landscapes.

Sadly, there are few examples of mini-

mally disturbed natural landscapes remaining. However, due to the efforts of some far-seeing individuals and organizations such as The Nature Conservancy, there are still, in many regions of the country, representative examples of naturally evolved landscapes which can provide both information and inspiration.

During the past 15 years I have taught field courses that deal with the composition, structure and aesthetic characters of native plant communities. These experiences have convinced me of two things: (1) there is great value in studying natural landscapes and native plants in the field, where one can hear, see, smell, touch and even taste them; and (2) the natural landscapes for study and enjoyment are more critical than ever as more and more of our land is "developed."

Lessons from Nature

An important concept is the presence of *plant communities* or *associations* of plants that frequently occur together under specific environmental conditions within a particular region. When these associations have not been greatly disrupted by human activity, there is an order and a visual harmony present, resulting from the fitness of the plants to that environment.

A plant community may be defined as "a group of plants living at a particular place at a particular time." Plant communities

DARREL G. MORRISON *is dean of the School of Environmental Design at the University of Georgia, Athens, GA.*

may be identified by some of the key species in them (e.g., the oak-hickory forest, the beech-maple forest), or by their environmental characteristics (e.g., the floodplain forest, the sandy ridge forest). Rarely is a plant community a sharply defined entity. Instead, one community may grade almost imperceptibly into another. Nevertheless, the plant community provides a framework within which we can approach the design of natural appearing gardens. Several characteristics of naturally evolved plant communities are useful as a basis for designing naturalistic gardens:

1. SPECIES COMPOSITION. A good starting point is to determine the key species that occur together in a specific environment; for example, on a dry, south-facing slope with rocky soil or on a moist, north-facing slope with deep, rich soil. Learn what the *dominant* species are; that is the major plants that have the greatest influence on the community. In a forest, the dominant species are typically the canopy or overstory trees. In a prairie, they are the grasses.

Next, learn which species are most *abundant* or *prevalent*; that is the ones that occur in greatest numbers, whether they are the canopy trees, the middle-story trees and shrubs, or the ground-layer vegetation. Then, learn additional species which are critical to the visual character of the community. They may be species with distinctive branching, flowering or outstanding fall color that makes them important visually in the natural model *and* hence, in designed landscapes based on that community. I refer to these as the "visual essence" species.

2. PLANT DISTRIBUTION PATTERNS. With an understanding of the most important species in a plant community, the next step is to observe the distribution of each species. There are two different aspects to plant distribution within a community: (a) the species' distribution relative to micro-climates (Does a plant grow only at the edge of the woods, does it grow only on the interior, or both? Does a plant grow only on the upper, drier slopes, or on the lower, moister slopes, or both?); and (b) the species' characteristic degree of aggregation or "clumping" (Does the species usually grow as an individual, or in loose colonies, or dense clumps?). Knowledge of the distribution of a species in a plant community has obvious implications for planting that species in a designed setting.

Some of the above information can be obtained from books or other publications. Or it may sometimes be obtained from local botanists, but the best way to learn it is through first-hand observation, preferably with someone who is familiar with the regional vegetation.

3. NATURAL ORDER. In undisturbed natural landscapes, we often sense an order or unity that is missing from the human-dominated environment. Natural order is not a simplistic, orchardlike order. Instead, it is a subtle order that results from the repetition of lines, forms, colors and textures within a particular plant community. For example, in a temperate North American forest, limited numbers of tree species will dominate the canopy level. In the Midwestern prairies, 90% of the vegetation is comprised of five or six grasses with their fine textures unifying the landscape.

4. VARIETY AND DIVERSITY. While there is visual harmony or unity resulting from the limited array of species within a specific environment, there is also visual variety and diversity. For example, while the tree canopy may be made up of a half-dozen species in a woodland, the ground layer beneath may typically include nine to twelve species per square meter. And while the prairie is mainly composed of fewer than 10 species, there may well be an additional 50 or 60 species-per-acre occurring in small numbers. Additionally, visual diversity results from varied spacing and different ages and sizes of plants within an

area. Ephemeral qualities, such as changing flower and foliage displays, also contribute seasonal diversity.

5. SPACES AND EDGES. The shape of natural open spaces provides useful guidance for designing spaces. In nature, the river provides one of the most useful analogies for garden designers. A river winds through a landscape, widening at turns or bends, and disappearing behind "peninsulas" of vegetation. This provides an element of mystery, encouraging the observer to want to see what's beyond the next bend.

Enclosing vegetation usually has younger, shorter shrubs at the front edge. Also, rather than a continuous, consistent wall of enclosing vegetation, there are individuals or clumps of plants advancing into the open space, and points where the space penetrates into the enclosing vegetation. The result is a softness to the edges in nature, unlike the hard edges we see in urban settings.

Designing the Garden Using Natural Principles

The naturalistic gardens we design are simplifications and stylizations of the natural landscapes they emulate. Yet they can have the "essence" of nature about them, particularly over time.

Here are some steps in the design of a naturalistic garden, and some suggestions of ways the lessons we've learned from nature can be applied:

SITE ANALYSIS. An important first step is to gain an understanding of the environmental characteristics of the proposed garden site. For example, determine the soil type(s), sun/shade distribution, relative moisture and existing vegetation. In regard to existing vegetation, we need to know both the plants that are undesirable and therefore may need to be suppressed or removed, and the desirable plants that will contribute to a natural appearing landscape. A "purist" philosophy suggests removal of any exotic species; in reality, compromises may need to be made.

MASS-SPACE PLAN. The next step is to develop the spatial form of the garden. There will almost certainly be a pathway or system of open spaces in a garden. The form of these might well emulate the river with its gentle to sweeping curves, and its partially concealed spaces. The "river of space" may be translated into a pathway surface, or a mulched area or lawn (acknowledging that the garden is a stylized form of nature). Next, lay out zones of vegetation within different height ranges; for example, ground-layer plants below three feet in height; middle-story shrubs and small trees in the three to fifteen feet height range; and taller, canopy trees. Laying out these zones—on paper and/or on the ground—will be very helpful to provide the "structure" of the garden.

PLANT SELECTION. The next step in the design is to select the plant species for the different height zones of the plan. With an understanding of environmental conditions on the site and of the needs of the native plant communities in a region, you can simply select species from the appropriate community(ies) for the native garden. In general, the closer you adhere to this principle, the more likely you will be to have a unified, harmonious garden. But there may be situations in which exotic species are selected; for example, to expand the blooming period. Some precautions to doing that: (1) avoid introducing species whose flowers will overpower the native species; and (2) always avoid plants that have been known to get out of hand and invade surrounding natural areas. Purple loosestrife (*Lythrum salicaria*) is a prime example of such an aggressive species.

PLANT PLACEMENT. Having selected a palette of plants for a naturalistic garden, arranging those plants within their respective zones is the next step. A simple but effective approach is to delineate the different vegetation zones, and then use

Along the East Coast the major plant communities are forests, such as the evergreen Spruce-Fir Community of high altitudes and latitudes and Pine-Oak-Hickory Communities at lower altitudes and latitudes.

The golden leaves of birch dominate this autumn scene in New York State.

color-coded stakes to locate individual plants within each zone. While it is unlikely that you can initially plant at the same density as nature does, the same principles of distribution can be followed; for example, "drifts" of some species may flow through the zone; other species that occur as individuals in nature may be distributed similarly in the garden. There may well be spaces between plants or drifts of plants which are mulched, providing an environment for the natural spread of the initially planted vegetation.

In the case of meadow-or prairie-like plantings, zones may be identified for different seed mixes, rather than for the placement of individual plants.

At edges, where plants meet the pathway or open spaces, the slightly undulating, irregular edges of nature may be emulated through the plants' placement.

CHANGE OVER TIME. Just as a natural landscape is ever-changing, so is a naturalistic garden. In fact, one of the great rewards of naturally based design is that it will change as plants increase and "migrate" into hospitable niches. In the early years of a naturalistic garden's evolution, it is particularly important to watch for intrusions or reappearances of aggressive exotic species that may take over. Also, as conditions change; for example, as more shade develops, additional plants or seeds may be introduced, and others will be shaded out. Finally, in order to perpetuate the composition, selective removal or pruning may be necessary.

Summary

Natural appearing landscapes do not "just happen" in our previously disturbed environment. But they can be designed, planted and managed so that they resemble the natural landscapes which inspired them. Studies of relatively undisturbed natural landscape provide one of the best ways to learn principles of design that can be incorporated into the gardens. 🐾

SPIDERWORT
(Tradescantia)

ILLUSTRATION BY NETTIE S. SMITH

MAINTAINING THE NATURALISTIC GARDEN

RICHARD W. LIGHTY

The maintenance of gardens is often held to be a tedious and mindless job. It is regarded as something apart from the making of gardens, and this may be true for some public or commercial landscapes; but fine gardening demands continuing personal involvement of the garden maker, not only in planting and renewal, but in the routine care. Gardening is a dynamic art; the product of natural growth and the gardener's wishes, and maintenance is the choreography of inevitable change, daily, seasonally and through the years. Seen in this light, garden maintenance is a creative and enjoyable process which fine tunes the garden to the taste of the gardener.

The tasks involved in garden maintenance are the same for all types of gardens, but the particular approach to accomplishing the task depends on the style of the garden and the preferences of the gardener. Gardens, even naturalistic ones, differ from nature in two important ways:

they require a higher level of interest through the seasons and they require that plants grow in sites we, not they, have chosen. These are also the major reasons maintenance is required. I can't resist adding that this effort is considered a pleasant pastime by a large portion of our population.

The basic tasks of garden maintenance are: the control of undesirable and desirable vegetation; the removal of dead or dying plant parts; and provision for the plants' needs for water or nutrients.

Weeding — The Control of Unwanted Vegetation

There is a variety of approaches to this oldest of tasks and thoughtful gardeners will consider which is most appropriate in each situation. Hand-pulling of weeds, roots and shoots is the most certain and precise. Its disadvantages are in the time it takes and the necessity of stooping or kneeling. It also disturbs the soil which brings new weed seeds to the surface where they quickly germinate. Despite this, it is often the quickest method of eliminating non-rhizomatous weeds from tight ornamental plantings, but it will never eradicate established weeds with extensive rhizomes or sprouting root systems.

Tools and machines such as hoes, cultivators and hand weeders need more room in which to operate than do fingers, but

RICHARD W. LIGHTY *received his Ph.D. from Cornell University in plant breeding and genetics. In 1966, he joined the Plant Science Department of the University of Delaware and administered the Longwood Graduate Program training horticulturists for managerial roles in public gardens. In 1983, he became director of Mt. Cuba Center in Greenville, DE, a garden emphasizing plants native to the Piedmont region. Native plants are featured in one section of his seven-acre home garden which he has developed over the past 25 years.*

Candelabra primroses, although not native, make a pretty scene
in a naturalistic garden along a Connecticut streambank.

they cover the ground more quickly. They also disturb the soil, bringing a new crop of seeds to the surface and they destroy fine feeder roots of desirable plants. Power cultivators have limited use in established naturalistic gardens, but there are places where hoes and hand weeders can hasten the task without creating a problem. Where plants like trilliums or Christmas fern have a wide "overhang" to shade the soil, hand tools can be used to scratch the surface without increasing the weed problem.

The final method of controlling established weeds is with herbicides. The term encompasses a variety of chemicals that can be dangerous to humans and other organisms that share our environment. Care should be taken to use the least hazardous ones in the safest possible way. Always follow the label directions. Herbicides should be used only when they represent the sole practical means of control. In general, I do not advocate the use of persistent, soil-acting herbicides such as the pre-emergence types in common use on some nurseries and farms. All herbicides must be carefully applied at the correct rate. The types I recommend are those absorbed by the green tissues, such as leaves, and subsequently translocated throughout the plant, killing it slowly and surely. Somewhat less useful are those that kill only the green parts touched by the spray. In the first group we have types which are *selective* and can be sprayed on all vegetation but kill only certain types. The most common of these are 2,4-D and related compounds which kill broad-leaved plants without injuring most grasses. For the naturalistic gardener these can be helpful in keeping meadows weed-free by spot-spraying only the areas of infestation. They will, however, injure or kill broad-leaved ornamentals in the same area if they drift or volatilize excessively. There are several recent additions to the arsenal of herbicides which kill grasses but do not injure most broad-leaved plants (e.g. Poast™, Fusilade™. These, when labeled for use with ornamentals, will be useful where rhizomatous grasses are a problem.

Non-selective, translocated herbicides must be sprayed only on the target weed. Glyphosate (e.g. Roundup™, Kleenup™, Rodeo™) is the most common of these and can be very effective when "dribbled" at low pressure from a sprayer or applied by moist sponge. These methods, if carefully used, will avoid any splash or accidental application to desirable plants. For concentrations and restrictions, always consult the label.

The single most important purpose of any weed control measure is to kill weeds before they go to seed (in the case of annuals or biennials) or before their rhizomes or root systems spread throughout the planting (in the case of perennials). By eliminating them when they are small you have the additional advantage of less soil disturbance.

Much effort can be avoided by having all soil covered with either vegetation or leaflitter so that small weed seedlings can't get started. Gardeners in public gardens with naturalistic plantings have for years used shredded oak leaves as a mulch applied in early winter. If the leaves are chopped to a size of about one and one-half inch, they will settle in to provide a loose blanket, reducing frost heaving of shallow-rooted plants and preventing the germination of weed seeds. The size and looseness allows established plants to come through without problems. Leaf chopping can be done at the time of leaf removal in the fall. Some vacuums (e.g. Roof™) chop and bag as they remove, but hand-raked leaves may be chopped by repeatedly running over the pile with a lawn mower set as high as possible. Oak leaves are the best, but others may be used as long as care is taken to keep the soil pH suitable to the plants being grown. Heavy, leathery leaves should be avoided as mulch.

While its use is restricted by social and safety considerations, the periodic use of fire can help in the maintenance of meadows and certain very specific woodland gardens. Those who feel it might be appropriate should check with their local authorities and with experts in nearby public gardens regarding legal limitations and horticultural advisability. Mowing or use of a string trimmer is an alternative to burning but does not kill weed seeds and seedlings as fire can.

The Control of Beneficial Vegetation

Once the garden has developed as planned, the gardener will be in the enviable position of spending more time controlling the desirable plants than fending off invaders. But it still takes time, and the following approaches will ease the task.

Select your herbaceous plants carefully, not only for aesthetic attributes, but to avoid excessively invasive plants. In general, gardeners who let bishop's goutweed (*Aegopodium podagraria*)*, yellow archangel (*Lamiastrum galeobdolon*)*, gooseneck loosestrife (*Lysimachia clethroides*)* or their like into the naturalistic garden, will live to regret it. Also know what you are doing when you plant garden phlox (*Phlox paniculata*), foxglove (*Digitalis purpurea*)*, fountain grass (*Pennisetum alopecuroides*)* or others that seed themselves profusely. While the methods outlined for weed control apply generally to the control of ornamentals, translocated herbicides should not be used on the latter unless you wish to eliminate the plant entirely.

Even those plants that are clump formers may spread fast enough to become a threat and all will ultimately need division and resetting if they are well cared for. Plants should be carefully selected and spaced so that the ground is covered in a year or two and still permit the plant to grow for five to ten years before needing division. Since rate of growth is affected by many factors, each gardener must experiment to arrive at the best approach for a particular site. The usual mistake is to plant too closely so as to produce a quick effect, and this necessitates frequent division. Gardeners should carry pruning shears and constantly trim back the edges of vigorous plantings to keep them from overgrowing less hearty neighbors.

The control of desirable woody plant growth is more straightforward. The most important requirement is for gardeners to understand the growth habits of their plants; where long growth occurs, where buds which give rise to new shoots are found, what the effect will be of removing a particular shoot, and what the ultimate size and character of the plant will naturally be. One is then equipped to direct growth in ways that allow all the plants to fit harmoniously into the garden. In general, prune small amounts, do it frequently and begin early in the plant's life. Prune throughout the year, being careful not to remove large portions of the plant in late summer when the resultant new growth will be less winter hardy. Large-scale pruning should be done in mid-winter. When tampering with the canopy, the upper layers of branches in a woodland, gardeners should not be tempted to let too much light in too quickly. This will increase all growth and bloom in the under-stories, including that of weedy species. After all, naturalistic gardens need not strive for the bloom of a formal bed of annuals. When thinning the canopy, remove branches throughout the crown of the trees, not just at the bottom (limbing up) or storm breakage and blowdowns will result. Another rule: Never alter the natural form of the tree or shrub drastically. The eye will read this as artificial.

The Removal of Dead or Dying Litter

Leaf removal is as essential in a woodland garden with an herbaceous layer as mowing is in a meadow. Without it plants are smothered and reduced in size and diversity. Raking is the simplest, most careful way of removing fallen leaves, but it also is the most time consuming. If you have an area of any size, consider a large-wheeled leaf vacuum which chops and bags the leaves as it removes them. As mentioned before, the leaves can then be compactly piled nearby for return to the same area as mulch in early winter. A pitchfork is ideal for putting on a light and airy cover. Try to wait until rodents have found homes elsewhere before putting the leaves back, although chopped leaves make less desirable cover for these furry foes than do whole leaves. Other, more expensive mulches can be used, but none have the natural look of leaf litter. Bed cleanup can be done as the leaves are removed, but many gardeners enjoy the brown seedheads as an important part of the winter garden. Because of the complexity of a naturalistic garden, bed cleanup requires close attention and hand work, although a skillfully used weed whip can make tasks such as the removal of old flowering stems easier.

Provision for Basic Needs

Again, because any garden is unnatural to the extent that it is a garden, input is constantly required to keep the site as desired. By putting more plants of more sorts in an area than would be found there naturally, we come up against the problem of limiting factors. Whereas in a natural forest, many herbaceous plants go dormant at the onset of mid-summer drought, the gardener strives to maintain contrived effects of texture, form and green throughout the season. Since there are more plants in a given area than nature usually supports and, since aesthetics-conscious gardeners use moisture-requiring plants in unnaturally dry sites, water becomes limited and must be supplied from sources other than rainfall. While overhead sprinklers have traditionally been used because of their flexibility, they are wasteful of water and can abet the spread of foliage diseases and rots. A new generation of trickle irrigation

devices and soaker hoses promises less waste, but these, if installed for a season, have problems of unsightliness in a naturalistic garden and lack flexibility as the garden grows and changes. A general rule for watering, if you must, is to do it as soon as the need becomes evident (not critical), and do it in the very early morning. In normal years watering should not be a major time-consuming task if your garden is planned properly. Burying seasonal water lines before you plant the garden will decrease the need to carefully thread hoses through prized plantings.

Nitrogen becomes a limiting factor in somewhat the same way. Most of us can easily see when a plant is thriving, and we know that "fertilizer" makes this happen. Indeed, we tend to supply too much nitrogen and this has a number of troublesome consequences. It may delay or reduce flowering make the plant more disease and drought susceptible and by increasing soft vegetative growth, can shorten the life of perennial plants or at least the length of time before they need division. Moderation in the application of all fertilizers should be the rule. I do not fertilize any plantings unless they show signs of deficiency for some element. Usually this is nitrogen, and I correct it with a half-cup of 5-10-10 per square yard. Light fertilization and watering will also help many of the spring ephemerals, such as bleeding heart (*Dicentra eximia*), corydalis (*Corydalis lutea*) and bloodroot (*Sanguinaria canadensis*), remain green later into the summer.

Several things the gardener can do at the beginning will have a salutary effect on garden maintenance. Burying water and electric lines in convenient spots throughout the garden is one of those. Electrical tools are often lighter, usually less expensive and have fewer moving parts and a lower repair frequency than their gasoline counterparts. For the home gardener they make sense. Design of the garden for maximum path frontage (consistent with the overall aesthetic design) will allow the gardener to plant for higher interest while maintaining less total area. It is the intimate and varied combinations near the path that add delight to the garden. An overall plan at the start will enable the gardener not only to bury utilities and lay out paths, but to phase garden development so that only as much area as can be cared for will be in a disturbed state at any time. As each area matures, the gardener can advance into another. This slow development also allows the gardener to accomplish disruptive tasks like thinning trees, removing shrubs and placing stones before planting, and to gain experience in maintenance and correct early mistakes before embarking into a new area. Unimproved areas can be left as nature leaves them or mowed and kept weed free until you are ready to plant. The alternative is to be endlessly engulfed in tall weeds that must be hand pulled.

Finally, it is hoped that this brief treatment of the most time-consuming (and the least considered) aspect of gardening will inspire gardeners to look at the vexing problems of maintenance with the confidence that by analyzing their particular situation and applying appropriate technology to the basic tasks involved, the care of their garden will become as pleasant as its making.

*Editor's note: These plants are not U.S. natives.

Some Rules of Thumb

1. Don't change conditions in ways that increase maintenance unless the trade-off is worth it.

EXAMPLES: Clearing out brush or opening the canopy increases bloom and the variety of plants you can grow, but it also increases weeds and weed growth. Shade gardens are peaceful in more ways than one.

Aquilegia canadensis pokes through a picturesque bench at the Mt. Cuba Center in Delaware.

Tilling the earth for planting also provides a fertile field for weeds and brings weed seeds to the surface. Limit the amount of disturbed and bare ground by the energy you have to care for it. In a naturalistic garden, living plants and dead litter are the desirable surface covers.

2. Plant for permanence - a function of the plant's persistence within the bounds you have assigned it. An ideal planting will neither overgrow its neighbors nor decline noticeably in vigor over five to ten years so that it needs restoration. Your own experience is the best guide.

EXAMPLES: Use slow-growing, long-lived, clumping plants in combination with lower, shade-tolerating ground covers to control weeds. For example, trilliums or merrybells (*Uvularia grandiflora*) planted with *Phlox stolonifera*.

Use slow-growing shrubs and trees. They take longer to achieve their effect, but require less control over their long life. A silver maple will provide shade in five years but will threaten the house in another ten, while a white oak will take ten years to give much shade, but will be a solid and well-behaved specimen for several hundred years.

3. Combine tasks to avoid handling materials or reworking unnecessarily.

EXAMPLES: Fall leaf removal can be combined with mulching if a leaf vacuum/chopper is used.

Weeding, dead-heading and summer pruning can all be done simultaneously. Make several "sweeps" through the garden each summer and carry with you the tools to do all routine tasks.

4. Look hardest at those tasks demanding most time or effort. A small savings here means much more than a large savings in a trivial task.

EXAMPLES: A technique which reduces weeding time in a newly-planted ground cover is more worthwhile than completely solving the small weed problem

existing after it is established.

Contouring the lawn edges to fit the radius-of-turn of your mower will save a large amount of time spent in hand trimming. It will probably save more than that gained by using string-trimmers or trim mowers in the same area.

5. Try to eliminate tasks that consume even small amounts of time each week or each year, if that task must be repeated endlessly.

EXAMPLES: Careful, slow application of a foliar-applied, translocatable herbicide, to Canada thistle growing in a ground cover will put an end to pulling it or digging it several times a summer, year after year.

Removal of all broadleaved weeds in the lawn adjacent to beds at the same time these weeds are removed from the beds will prevent the back and forth seeding from one area to the other. In a few years you will notice fewer weeds in both areas. 🌱

A Connecticut woodland walk in spring with foamflower and *Chrysogonum virginianum* in full bloom.

37

DESIGNING WITH NATIVE PLANTS

Darrel G. Morrison

The new, or newly revived, interest in designing with native plants—trees, shrubs, vines, wildflowers, ferns and grasses—presents a whole new series of challenges to the landscape architect. The purposes of this article are: to identify some of the differences between traditional landscape design as it is currently being practiced and new forms of design that rely more heavily on the use of native vegetation and natural processes; and to suggest ways in which naturally evolving landscapes may serve as models for designing landscapes that are both ecologically sound and aesthetically satisfying.

Current Practices

Before discussing the range of potential approaches and techniques for designing with native vegetation in ways that depart to some degree from current landscape design practice, it is appropriate to review those practices as seen in present-day planting design. This discussion is a generalized view and does not take into consideration many individual variations, but it does provide a basis for comparison.

Designing with plants—whether in a traditional mode or in the alternative native landscape approaches—involves two major components: selection of plants and placement of them in the landscape.

PLANT SELECTION. In typical contemporary landscape design, plant selection is primarily influenced by:

1. AESTHETIC CHARACTERISTICS such as the forms, texture and seasonal color characteristics of plants.

2. FUNCTIONAL CAPABILITIES such as the capacity of plants to provide shade, windbreaks, enclosure, visual screens and erosion control.

3. ENVIRONMENTAL TOLERANCES such as cold hardiness; drainage requirements; sun, shade and wind tolerance; and, in some urban areas, the ability to survive the effects of pollutants in the soil and atmosphere. The moisture requirements of plants are characteristically given only secondary consideration, because of the relative ease, up to now, of providing regular or periodic supplemental water to plants that require more water than precipitation provides.

4. COMMERCIAL AVAILABILITY. A very real consideration in plant selection is the availability or non-availability of a plant species. Plant producers, especially the large nurseries, tend to mass-produce large quantities of a relatively small number of species that are well known and reliable. They typically include both native and exotic species, as well as hybrids and cultivars; and for the most part, the plants' origins are not clearly differentiated.

Similarly, there is in typical landscape design today little attempt to select a native over a non-native species, if both have similar aesthetic attributes or functional capabilities. For example if designers were looking for a canopy tree with showy yellow fall foliage color for a site in hardiness Zone 4, they are probably as likely to select a *Ginkgo biloba* (ginkgo) from eastern China as a *Fraxinus pennsylvanica* (green ash), whose natural range is central and eastern North America (Wyman, 1951).

Generally, in selecting mid-story trees and shrubs, there is a tendency to select plant species with at least one outstanding aesthetic attribute, such as showy flowers, brilliant fall color or conspicuous fruit. Evergreen shrubs are particularly valued. This is evidenced by the number of conifers such as *Juniperus chinensis pfitzeriana* (Pfitzer juniper); *Taxus cuspidata* (Japanese yew); broad-leaved evergreens such as *Ilex* (holly); and *Photinia serrulata* (red-tipped photinia) in the designed landscapes of different parts of the country.

Similarly, in the selection of ground covers, there is a strong tendency to choose repeatedly a few species that are green all year round. One of the most widespread ground covers in designed landscapes is *Hedera helix* (English ivy). Other frequently

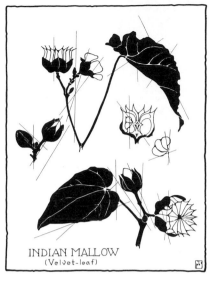

INDIAN MALLOW
(Velvet-leaf)

selected ground covers include *Vinca minor* (periwinkle or myrtle) and *Pachysandra terminalis* (Japanese spurge). All of these were introduced from Europe or Asia more than a century ago (Wyman, 1949).

Of course the most widely used ground-cover plants in contemporary-designed landscapes are the sod-forming lawn grasses, which are almost without exception exotic species and are typically maintained with substantial inputs of fertilizers, herbicides, water and energy (Diekelmann and Schuster, 1982).

Since neither the lawn grasses nor the other ground covers display conspicuous flowers, color at the ground-layer level is typically provided by seasonal displays of bulbs and annuals.

PLANT PLACEMENT. Just as plant selection tends toward simplicity and order, so do the current practices of plant distribution or placement in the designed landscapes.

Trees are often planted as individual specimens in lawns, or in rows that reflect the geometry of surrounding buildings and streets in urban areas. In larger parks and on institutional grounds, they may be grouped in borders and islands, often spaced 25 to 30 feet apart, with all trees in a group of a single species and size.

Shrubs may be used singly as accents. More frequently, they are grouped with other members of the same species, equally spaced in rows or mulched beds. Either in a conscious effort to give shrubs an architectonic form or to keep them from outgrowing their situation, they are clipped, creating either square or rounding

39

Chrysogonum virginianum is a good choice for light shade.

forms that are dense and compact.

Ground-covering plants are generally spaced closely, at six to twelve inches apart, for a quick, uniform cover. Again, one species is typically used within a specific area in such plantings. Beds of ground-cover plants are usually clearly differentiated from lawn areas and other ground-cover beds, delineated by sunken steel edging or other materials that lead to distinct edges.

Bulbs and annuals, when used, are characterstcally planted as solid masses for maximum color effect, although bulbs such as *Narcissus* species may be naturalized in areas covered with a mulch or planted with other ground covers.

Contemporary traditional landscape management is geared to leaving both the species composition and distribution patterns of plants unchanged. Invading plants are removed, and reproduction of the initially planted individuals is inhibited.

Where feasible, existing trees are often preserved and incorporated into designed landscapes, sometimes at great expenditures of effort and money. Such trees, individually or in groups, tend to provide a link with the region's natural environment. Interestingly, though, where groups of trees are preserved, there is a strong tendency to clear out middle-story and ground-layer species, replacing them with the "cleaner" look of lawns, mulch beds, or monotypic blankets of ground cover such as English ivy.

Differences in cold and heat tolerance lead to some variations in the palette of plants used in different regions. Differing moisture requirements, on the other hand, are often accommodated through irrigation, making it possible to grow plants from a moderate to high rainfall region in an arid or semi-arid environment, or to grow plant species from natural lowland habitats in upland situations.

In summary, one of the effects of much of the current practice in planting design is to produce landscapes that have less and less resemblance to the natural landscape of the region in which they occur. At the same time, the designed landscape of one region tends to resemble more and more the designed landscapes of other regions.

Aesthetically, the prevailing contemporary-designed landscape tends to be ordered, with smooth green lawns interspersed by predominantly dense and dark green shrubs planted as hedges or in masses and symmetrically shaped trees planted either as individual specimens or in rows or groups composed of individuals of the same size and species. The only visible changes that are noticeable in this landscape are changing foliage colors of some of the trees and the changing displays of bulbs and annuals.

Natural Alternatives

In contrast to the relatively predictable, orderly and static landscapes that are products of typical planting design, there is a wide range of landscape possibilities that incorporate plant species native to the region and the microhabitat type in which they are planted. We might portray these potential approaches on a continuum that increasingly departs from standard landscape design practices and progressively incorporates natural processes as well as native materials. Following are steps along that continuum, indicating approaches that might be followed in different contexts by a landscape architect.

Substitution of native species of trees, shrubs and vines for the more commonly used mix of natives, exotics and cultivars represents a first step in the continuum. For example, this might suggest using a native *Viburnum* species in place of the exotic *Photinia* species in a shrub group, or a native *Amelanchier* species in place of an Oriental cherry. With this approach, plant selection has been modified, but placement is similar to that in a conventional design. There is a tendency to have greater continuity with the surrounding natural landscape of the region because of the repetition of similar species. Furthermore, if the plants are placed in appropriate microhabitats, there is less need for supplemental watering, feeding and protection from temperature extremes than there would be for many of the introduced species.

The next step along the continuum might be the introduction of a diverse mix of native ground-layer species in appropriate microhabitats, replacing the mulch beds and monotypic ground cover and annual flower beds that are so abundantly used in standard landscape design today. The forms of mulch or ground-cover beds might remain very much the same, but the species makeup would change. For example, in a shaded area English ivy might be replaced by a mix of ferns and woodland wildflowers; in a sunny flower bed, a mix of native meadow or prairie perennials might replace the sequence of spring bulbs, summer annuals and fall chrysanthemums. Finally, the exotic irrigation-requiring lawn

Fothergilla major puts on a dramatic fall display.

might be replaced by a native sod former, such as *Buchloe dactyloides* (buffalo grass) in some of the Great Plains states. Again, even though the design form may not differ significantly from that in conventional contemporary landscape design, the ground-layer planting, like the trees and shrubs in the scenario discussed previously, will bear some relation to the region's natural landscape and should result in reduced input of water, fertilizer and specialized management and maintenance procedures.

A third level of complexity in the continuum of natural alternatives is the utilization of communitylike groupings of native vegetations as design elements. At this point along the continuum, both the selection and placement of plants are related to the species composition and distribution patterns that occur in the natural landscape. Following this approach, in the portions of a designed landscape where three-dimensional mass and enclosure are among the design objectives, one might initiate a planting that will emulate the

41

natural forest for the region and the specific habitat type, utilizing the most characteristic canopy, middle-story, and ground-layer species of that forest type in the planting. Because such plantings would rarely be equivalent in size or extent to the natural stands of that forest type, the species array in the planting might similarly be scaled down. But the key species, the plant density, and distribution patterns would ideally capture the essence of the natural model over time. Similarly, in meadowlike or prairielike plantings in sunny areas, the composition would ideally incorporate the visually important species, the characteristic grass, forb ration and distribution patterns in a naturally evolved meadow or prairie. The stylized, abstracted plant community groupings included in this approach might be used as borders and islands adjacent to mowed lawns in some contexts. Hence, this approach is not a total re-creation of nature.

Ecosystem restoration, with a reintroduction of a full array of native species and reinitiation of natural processes on sites that have been adversely affected by earlier human activity, represents the most complex end of the continuum. Initially such work may require the reversal of some effects of this earlier activity; e.g., eradication of exotic and aggressive plant species or rebuilding of an organic soil where it has been removed. Next, propagules of an appropriate mix of species need to be reintroduced, sometimes over a period of years, and the restoration is managed in methods emulating natural processes.

Learning From Natural Models

Even using the most elementary approach to landscape design with native vegetation, the designer needs to know something about the local natural landscape. For example, in the approach described as the substitution model, with native species of trees and shrubs placed in a traditional design form, the designer needs to know what is native locally. Although certain information can be learned from the literature, there is no satisfactory substitute for carefully observing the naturally occurring native plant communities of a region, if there are any preserved remnants.

Examples of information that can be obtained through such observation may include the following:

SPECIES COMPOSITION. One can sometimes obtain lists of native plants for a particular geographic area, but they only become meaningful to the designer when those plants are seen in their community groupings. Even identification becomes easier when one observes a particular plant repeatedly in similar environments. Even if it is unrealistic to expect to learn all the plant species in a community type, it is possible to learn dominant species, such as the major canopy trees in a forest community; prevalent species, which are those that occur with the greatest frequency; and visual essence species, those which may be important because of a distinctive aesthetic attribute (Morrison and Howell, 1983).

DISTRIBUTION PATTERNS. The distribution pattern of a particular species, as it occurs in nature, provides a very logical basis for placement of the same species in a designed landscape. Two aspects of distribution are particularly useful to observe: the distribution of a species relative to micro-environmental conditions and the degree of aggregation that is exhibited by the species.

One can learn through field observation which species have very narrow environmental amplitude (e.g., occurring only in very hot, dry situations or only in full sun) versus those which have a wide range of moisture or sunlight tolerance.

Besides these distribution tendencies, most plants exhibit a characteristic degree of aggregation. Plants are usually considered to exhibit one of the following three types of distribution: regular, random or aggregated (Curtis, 1959). Of these, it has been my observation that some degree of aggregation is the most frequently occurring pattern. The aggregation may be loose, as in the case of *Fagus grandifolia* (American beech) in the Midwestern beech-maple forest, or it may be much more highly aggregated, with many closely spaced individuals, as with *Betula nigra* (river birch) in the riverine forest of the same region.

Differing degrees of aggregation become particularly important in creating visible patterns in open prairie and marsh communities, where species that spread vegetatively typically form dense aggregations that feather out at the edge.

This phenomenon of having greater density toward the center of a group and more widely spaced individuals at the edges might be termed the drifing of a species.

AESTHETIC CHARACTERISTICS. The aesthetics of naturally evolving plant communities are also best observed in extant stands of those communities. Among the noteworthy aesthetic attributes of naturally evolving landscapes that might be incorporated into designed ones are: spatial configuration, clumping and drifting of species, softness of edges and transitional zones, and diversity of colors and textures.

A recurrent theme in natural landscapes is the flowing space, an open space that bends out of sight and tends to have a degree of mystery. This characteristic is most obvious when it is embodied in a flowing river that curves, but it may also occur as an open space in an upland site.

Clumps and directional drifts of plants are common phenomena in naturally evolving landscapes. Clumps occur particularly with vegetatively reproducing shrubs and herbaceous plants which spread outward from a central nucleus. Typically, plants at the edges of shrub groups that spread in this manner are progressively shorter than those in the center, providing a rounding

horizon. Drifts of one species often feather out and merge with a second or third species.

Edges between different species groups, then, tend to be indistinct. Where one community type meets another, there is frequently interpenetration, as where an oak-hickory forest meets a prairie in the Midwest.

The colors and textures of natural landscapes are often more subtle and more diverse than those of the standard designed landscape. Flowers in nature usually do not occur in the solid masses that tulips or geraniums occupy in the designed landscape. Except in a few cases, there are usually several species occurring together in nature, as in a prairie, where the bold colors of the forbs' flowers are filtered and made more subtle by the linear leaves of grasses. There are typically more seasonal changes of color in the natural landscape than in the traditionally designed one. Instead of the consistently green color of the designed landscape with its lawns and evergreen ground covers and shrubs, there are grasses that become dormant, subtle flower and seed head colors, and deciduous shrubs that change color and then lose their leaves. Texturally, the natural landscape exhibits greater variety than many designed landscapes because of the fine textures of ferns, grasses, hedges and rushes, and the bare twigs of deciduous shrubs, sometimes occurring as clumps or thickets.

COMMUNITY DYNAMICS. One of the most important lessons that can be learned from observation of natural landscapes is that they are always changing. There are often long-term successional changes occurring almost imperceptibly but also short-term changes resulting from phenomena such as an individual tree falling in the forest, an animal building a mound of fresh soil outside its burrow, or water changing levels in a marsh. Each of these phenomena provides information we need to know in

43

designing and managing landscapes that display the forms and processes of natural landscapes.

Conclusion

In this article, I've tried to compare standard approaches to planting design with a series of alternative approaches and also to suggest that the best classroom for learning how to design with native plants and plant communities is the natural landscape itself.

The design, installation and management of naturally based landscapes holds great potential to provide a greater variety of designed landscapes, landscapes that are resource-conserving and that perpetuate regional differences. To be successful, it is essential that their designers understand not only artistic principles but also natural forms and processes. In the end, the ecological design may also be the most artful. 🌿

Literature Cited

Curtis, J. T. 1959. *The Vegetation of Wisconsin.* Madison, WI: University of Wisconsin Press

Diekelmann, J., and R. Schuster: 1982. *Natural Landscaping.* New York: McGraw-Hill.

Morrison, D. G., and E. Howell. 1983. "Field Study of Native Plant Communities: An Intensive Summer Course." In *Proceedings, Council of Educators in Landscape Architecture Annual Conference,* 126-134. Utah State University, Logan.

Wyman, D. 1949. *Shrubs and Vines for American Gardens.* New York: MacMillan.

Wyman, D. 1951. *Trees for American Gardens.* New York: MacMillan.

REPRINTED WITH PERMISSION FROM: *WILDFLOWER,* VOL. 1 (1) 13-18; THE PUBLICATION OF THE "NATIONAL WILDFLOWER RESEARCH CENTER," AUSTIN, TEXAS.

Phlox stolonifera 'Sherwoods Purple'at the Mt. Cuba Center. Woodland phlox makes an excellent ground cover. It has neat evergreen foliage just a few inches high and bears a profusion of flowers in May.

GREAT AMERICAN SMALL FLOWERING TREES:

TEN ALTERNATIVES TO BRADFORD PEARS

BOB HYLAND

Cercis canadensis

Trees between 20 and 40 feet in height with colorful flowers, fruit, bark and autumn foliage are in demand. Exotic species from the Orient such as magnolias, flowering cherries, crabapples, and Bradford pears have

BOB HYLAND *was visitor education specialist at Longwood Gardens, Kennett Square, PA for seven years. During that time, he taught courses on small flowering trees. He has masters degrees in ornamental horticulture from North Carolina State University and the University of Delaware. He is now a horticulturist in the San Francisco Bay area.*

been popular for decades. However, there are choice ornamental trees with multiseason interest that are native to North America and rival their foreign relatives. The following are ten examples.

Amelanchier arborea
(DOWNY SERVICEBERRY)

Several species of *Amelanchier* are confused in the nursery trade. Most are multistemmed shrubs, but *A. arborea,* native from Canada to Florida, Minnesota, Okla-

45

homa and Louisiana, grows into a tree 20-25 feet tall. It flowers for a short time (5-7 days) in mid- to late-April, but the pendulous clusters of white flowers are quite showy. Their weak fragrance is unpleasant to some.

A bonus for gardeners (and birds) are the edible fruits that ripen from green to red and finally purplish-black by June. The fruits are the size of miniature blueberries, but are not on the tree long enough to be ornamental.

Young leaves are covered with gray, downy fuzz when they first unfurl in the spring, but the hairiness disappears as the leaves reach full size. The foilage turns dramatic shades of yellow, orange, and deep red in autumn, making downy serviceberry one of the finest native trees for fall color. Vertical ridges and furrows of light and dark gray on the bark provide some winter interest.

Downy serviceberry is rarely used as a specimen tree and is, perhaps, more suitable in informal groupings in a lawn or mixed tree and shrub planting.

Hardy in Zones 4-9, tolerant of a wide range of soils and easy to cultivate, downy serviceberry is, unfortunately, prone to leaf rusts, powdery mildew, Japanese beetles, mites and aphids. An integrated program of sprays and good culture should yield healthy, attractive trees.

Asimina triloba
(PAWPAW)

Our native pawpaw is a small tree with unusual flowers and large leaves that have a tropical appearance. It generally grows as a multistemmed understory tree in woodlands from New York to Florida and west to Nebraska and Texas. When cultivated as a single-trunked tree, pawpaw merits attention for many gardens.

Pawpaw reaches 15-20 feet in height and naturally assumes a pyramidal shape when grown in full sun. Waxy, purple flowers in May often go unnoticed as the tree begins to leaf out. They are worth close inspection for their bizarre color and shape and they show off best in the small garden.

Coarse, 6- to 12-inch-long leaves turn an excellent yellow in autumn. They obscure small, edible, greenish yellow fruits that ripen to brown as they fall. The bananalike taste appeals to some people, and selections are being chosen for larger fruit and more distinctive taste.

A. triloba is hardy in Zones 5-8. It is ideal planted alone or in small groups. Native summer and fall-blooming perennials like New England aster *(Aster novae-angliae)*, Michaelmas daisy *(Aster cv.)*, goldenrods *(Solidago* spp.), ironweed *(Vernonia noveboracensis)* and Joe-Pye weed *(Eupatorium fistulosum)* make good companion plants. I have also seen a grove of pawpaws used effectively to define the edge of a parking lot at the Scott Arboretum on the Swarthmore College campus in Pennsylvania.

Trees prefer moist, fertile, slightly acid soils. They are difficult to transplant from the wild and should be purchased as balled-and-burlapped or container-grown stock. A word of caution! Pawpaws sucker from underground roots, but unwanted suckers are easily eliminated with a sharp spade or pruning shears.

Cercis canadensis
(EASTERN REDBUD)

Clusters of diminutive, rosy-pink flowers, heart-shaped leaves, and clear yellow autumn color characterize this small tree, hardy in Zones 5-9. It is an understory tree in woodlands from New Jersey to Florida, New Mexico and Texas. Taking a cue from its native habitat, plant redbuds in partial shade and either acid or alkaline, well-drained soils. Avoid lawnmower damage and improper pruning cuts which can provide entrance points for fungal organisms that cause cankers, a leading cause of branch dieback and plant death among redbuds.

The garden value of this tree is its lovely

flowering in mid-to late-April. Tiny blossoms that have the characteristic form of other plants in the Pea Family (garden beans and peas) are reddish-purple in bud and open to a lighter pink. Pealike pods, two to three inches long, develop after flowering and ripen from green to papery brown. Pods are more visible during the leafless dormant season, but have limited ornamental appeal.

Redbuds usually develop into multiple-stemmed, spreading, flat-topped trees that branch close to the ground. Judicious pruning at an early age can easily create a single-trunked specimen for patios and outdoor areas. Underplantings of Siberian squills (*Scilla sibirica*)*, lungworts (*Pulmonaria* spp.)*, moss pinks (*Phlox subulata* cultivars), or periwinkle (*Vinca minor*)* give nice effects.

A white-flowered form (*C. canadensis alba*) is sometimes observed in nature and is available from some nurseries. There are a few other native redbud species that are more suitable for other regions of the country. *C. reniformis* is native to Texas and New Mexico and has thicker leaves and deep pink flowers. California or western redbud (*C. occidentalis*) is native to California, Utah and Arizona. Its leaves are bright green and differ slightly in shape and size from its eastern relative. The purplish-pink blooms are also slightly larger.

Chionanthus virginicus
(FRINGE TREE)

Native from New Jersey south to Florida and west along the Gulf Coast to Texas, the fringe tree is an aristocrat in the garden. The plant is a multistemmed, shrubby tree with sparse branching. A mature specimen is 15-20 feet in height with an equal landscape spread.

Fringe tree shows little sign of life until mid-to late-spring. Then drooping, white flower clusters emerge at the same time as new leaves and quickly cover the trees with a haze of white fringe. On a gray, overcast day a fringe tree can seem to shimmer in the landscape.

Trees have male or female flowers but not both. Male flowers are larger in size and the dense clusters are slightly more showy than the bloom on female trees. However, choose females if you are interested in the small, bluish-black fruits shaped like small olives. They are attractive for several weeks in early fall. Otherwise, yellow leaf color is the only autumnal reward.

Give fringe trees fertile, acid soils on the moist side. They will grow either in full sun or partial shade and are effectively used in small groups in an open lawn or as specimens in a mixed herbaceous border.

In the mid-Atlantic and northeast regions, bloom time corresponds with tall bearded (*Iris* cv)* and Siberian irises (*I. siberica*)* and field poppies (*Papaver rhoeas*)*. The most dramatic tree I have seen is planted over a patio and studio garden near Wilmington, Delaware. Its springtime flowering and excellent summer shade are unbeatable.

Cornus alternifolia
(PAGODA DOGWOOD)

The landscape value of pagoda dogwood is its distinctive architectural form. Branches spread horizontally in tiers, suggestive of an oriental pagoda. It grows in the wild from Canada south to Georgia and Alabama and west to Minnesota and is hardy in Zones 3-7.

Flat-topped clusters of white flowers bloom in the spring from mid-to late-May and are somewhat malodorous. They are succeeded by blue-black, berrylike fruits held on pinkish-red stems. While colorful for awhile, the fruits are not long lasting.

C. alternifolia is a worthy substitute for its native relative, the eastern flowering dogwood (*C. florida*). Its showy white spring bracts, colorful red fruits, burgundy-red autumn foliage, pebbly bark texture, and easy propagation have made the eastern flowering dogwood one of the most handsome and popular small trees in North America. However, many have been killed by anthracnose, a fungal disease that first spots foliage and, if left unchecked, invades and kills stems, branches and entire trees.

Crataegus viridis
(GREEN HAWTHORN)

Green hawthorn, native from Virginia to Florida and west to Illinois, Missouri, and Texas, derives its common name from the greenish gray of its bark. Yet there are other reasons why this tree deserves more use in gardens.

It is outstanding for its heavy fruiting, rivaling many of the more popular crabapples. Clusters of reddish-orange fruits (each about one-quarter inch in diameter) ripen between September and October. The persistent fruits retain this bright color into the coldest winter months of January and February. A tree showing off its red fruits against a fresh blanket of snow is a sight to behold!

This 20- to 35-foot hawthorn develops a spreading, vase-shaped branching pattern. Stems and branches contain sharp, 1 1/2-inch-long thorns, a drawback to some gardeners.

Flowering comes in mid- to late-May and lasts seven to ten days. White flowers with five petals are borne in two-inch-wide clusters and exude an unpleasant scent.

C. viridis is hardy in Zones 5-9 and is easy to grow in full sun and most soil types. Its only problems are susceptibility to rusts that can spot and discolor leaves and fruits and, perhaps, a tendency to develop weak crotches and narrow branch angles that lead to splitting and structural damage on older trees.

A selection, *C. viridis* 'Winter King', is available and offers larger, deep red fruits. It and the species are among the best native trees for the winter landscape and garden.

Franklinia alatamaha
(FRANKLINIA)

If for no other reason, grow as a conversation starter. It was collected along the banks of the Altamaha River in Georgia in 1770 by John Bartram, but has never been seen in the wild since 1790. Supposedly, all plants available today are derived from Bartram's original collection.

More than a botanical curiosity, franklinia is a spectacular tree for some gardens and hardy in Zones 6-8. It rarely exceeds 20-25 feet in height and its multiple trunks spread to about 20 feet.

The real appeal of this tree is its late summer and fall bloom, generally early August in the mid-Atlantic and northeast regions. The cup-shaped, white petals enclose a distinctive cluster of yellow stamens and exude a faint fragrance. The flowers do not bloom all at once, but open sporadically from early August through September. Bloom may continue even after the shiny, dark green, 5- to 6-inch-long leaves have colored shades of orange, burgundy and scarlet in October.

Other ornamental features of franklinia are the hard, round, nutlike fruits that cling to branches after leaf drop. Smooth gray bark broken with lighter vertical fissures offers additional winter interest.

Franklinias thrive in moist, acid, well-drained soils suggestive of their lost, native coastal plain habitat. They develop sparse, fibrous root systems and are better purchased as small, container-grown plants. Larger balled-and-burlapped trees are not easily transplanted into the garden.

To take advantage of its summer flowering, combine franklinia with late-blooming ground covers like white lilyturf (*Liriope muscari* 'Monroe White')* or striking blue autumn leadwort (*Ceratostigma plumbaginoides*)*. Variegated carpet bugleweed (*Ajuga reptans* 'Burgundy Glow') or late-blooming hosta (*Hosta* 'Ginko Craig' or *H. plantaginea*)* are other possibilities.

Oxydendrum arboreum, sourwood, is most dramatic in fall when its three- to eight-inch-long leaves turn brilliant red and purple.

Halesia tetraptera
(CAROLINA SILVERBELL)
(incorrectly listed as *H. carolina*)

The diminutive, bell-shaped flowers of this small native tree are ephemeral but exquisite in the spring garden. It is seldom planted and deserves more attention.

The half inch, white bells develop in small clusters on year-old wood for one week in late April or early May. Suspended below branches, the flowers are best appreciated looking up into the tree canopy from underneath. A dark green background of conifers also accentuates the flowers when viewed from a distance.

Carolina silverbell is native to the East Coast from West Virginia to Florida and eastern Texas, and is hardy in Zones 5-8. Low, spreading branches form a broad, round crown. Mature landscape height is 30 to 40 feet, but the growth rate is no more than one foot per year.

Other ornamental attributes of this tree are its yellow fall leaves, papery brown four-winged fruits visible in fall and early winter, and ridged and furrowed bark alternating from light gray to brownish-black.

Silverbells transplant easily and prefer organic, acid soils. Full sun is best for flowering, but trees will tolerate partial shade. Carolina silverbell is a beautiful patio tree where its branches can spread horizontally and create an informal canopy. Pruning of lower branches will elevate the tree to a comfortable height for human activity below. Azaleas, rhododendrons and other broad-leaved evergreens are good companion plants. A ground cover of the native foamflower (*Tiarella cordifolia*) that blooms at the same time is one of the nicest plant combinations I have seen.

Magnolia virginiana
(SWEET-BAY)

Sweet-bay offers one of the most subtle, sweet, lemony-fresh fragrances among garden plants. Unlike its Oriental magnolia

in early spring, sweet-bay allows the competition to pass before blooming. The creamy white flowers with nine to twelve petals open over a four to six week period from late May to early July. Since the flowers are not produced in great abundance, they do not make a color statement when viewed from a distance. The cone-like fruits that split open to reveal bright red seeds in August are more distinctive.

In northern areas (Zones 5-7), *M. virginiana* forms a small, multistemmed, deciduous tree not more than 20 feet tall. In southern regions (Zones 8-9) sweet-bays are semievergreen to evergreen and form larger, pyramidal trees. Varieties of sweet-bay with better form and semievergreen foliage are being selected and tested for hardiness in northern climates.

Sweet-bay is an excellent tree for small patios, decks and open-air porches. Site a specimen near an open window to take full advantage of the sweet aroma that wafts lazily on summer breezes. The handsome, dark green leaves also provide interest when the wind buffets and exposes their silvery undersides. Unfortunately, the foliage provides no autumn color.

Sweet-bays tolerate wet soils, shade and acid soils. The shallow root systems develop near the soil surface and should be mulched to keep them cool and moist and to prevent disturbance from cultivation. Vigorous new stems occasionally grow at the base of sweet-bays, but are easily pruned out.

Oxydendrum arboreum
(SOURWOOD)

Sourwood is truly a tree for all seasons in home gardens in Zones 6-9. Michael Dirr in his *Manual of Woody Landscape Plants* says that "many gardeners feel, among native trees, this is second only to flowering dogwood" (*Cornus florida*). I think it is equal to or better than flowering dogwood.

Its habitat extends from Pennsylvania to Florida, and west to Indiana and Louisiana.

The tree naturally develops a pyramidal shape with drooping branches. It slowly grows to a maximum height of 30 feet in gardens and has a spread of 15 to 20 feet. A good plant for summertime bloom, sourwood sports drooping sprays of white flowers that cover a tree in a lacy veil from late June to early July. The tiny, individual urn-shaped blooms are reminiscent of lilies-of-the-valley.

During the remainder of the summer, flowers give way to yellowish-green fruiting capsules that gradually fade to brown. October may be the most dramatic time for sourwood when the lustrous dark green, three- to eight-inch-long leaves turn brilliant red and purple depending on weather conditions and siting. The sprays of tan fruits are dramatically accented by the vibrant foliage and provide winter interest after leaf drop.

Sourwoods are best transplanted as young trees. They demand acid soils (pH 5.5), perfect drainage and organic soils. A full sun exposure will ensure the best flowering and fall color. Heavy clay soils with poor drainage, drought and high pH lead to weak trees that never develop beautiful form or size.

Summer and fall-blooming perennials such as New England asters (*Aster novae-angliae*), daylily cultivars (*Hemerocallis*)*, black-eyed Susans (*Rudbeckia hirta*), and fall-blooming sunflowers (*Helianthus* x *multiflorus* 'Flore-Pleno') are potential combinations. Ornamental grasses are also ideal companions to sourwoods, especially variegated miscanthus (*Miscanthus sinensis* 'Variegatus')* and feather reed grass (*Calamagrostis acutiflora* 'Stricta')*.

Many of these native trees are available from local nurseries and mail-order companies. Check catalogs and ask your local garden center or nursery to order plants. These trees, while selected for small gardens, are ideal for all size gardens and will reward you with years of beauty. ❦

*Editor's Note: These plants are not U.S. natives.

GREAT AMERICAN SHRUBS

Harrison L. Flint

Temperate zone North American shrubs can be divided into two groups: those we use well in the landscape and those we don't. Over a third of our "standard" landscape shrubs have their origins somewhere in North America, the others originating from some other part of the world or from hybridization, accidental or deliberate. If we consider the richness of the woody flora of North America, we have to conclude that we are not using this reservoir of plants very well. That is the problem, and the opportunity, we face.

The shrubs that follow form a partial list of great natives that, in my opinion, are not used often enough, nor well enough, and the accompanying comments suggest ways of improving the situation. This list, arranged alphabetically by scientific name could be expanded greatly, given sufficient time and space, but let this sample serve as a start. Any native plant enthusiast can do the expanding, and no doubt each person's list will be unique.

AESCULUS PARVIFLORA (bottlebrush buckeye) is a great shrub for large-scale situations, with its pleasingly coarse foliage and solid visual mass. Add to that the spectacular flowering interest in midsummer, and it is hard to believe this plant is not used more often. Even the winter aspect of the plant is interesting, because of the tiered branching and upright, leftover flower stalks. Bottlebrush buckeye grows slowly when young and can be contained by pruning and digging-out sucker shoots in small-scale plantings, but it is most trouble-free, and perhaps most appropriately used, when massed in large plantings.

ARCTOSTAPHYLOS UVA-URSI (bearberry) is an extremely hardy shrub when well established, and establishment is usually not difficult if a few preparations are made. First, start with pot-grown plants that are not excessively potbound. Amend the soil as necessary to ensure it is well drained. Extra watering may be necessary for establishment, but keeping the soil waterlogged can kill bearberry plants quickly. During the first year after planting, avoid any fertilization of the soil other than super- or treble-phosphate in the planting mix, and powdered sulphur if the soil reaction (pH) is initially above 5.5 or so. It is not absolutely clear that this plant needs such acidic soil, but since it is a member of the Heath Family (Ericaceae), acidification is at least a good "hedge". When established in the right soil, this plant grows so vigorously that it will need to be contained in small-scale situations.

CORNUS AMOMUM (silky dogwood) is one of several species of more or less red-twigged shrubby dogwoods, including *Cornus sericea* (red-osier dogwood), another North American native. Silky dogwood is a little less cold-hardy than red-osier dogwood, and more adaptable to southern landscapes (to Zone 9a). Its twigs are not as bright red as those of red-osier dogwood in late winter, but its fruits ripen a beautiful blue in late summer or early autumn. It is equally useful for naturalized landscapes or

Oakleaf hydrangea, *Hydrangea quercifolia*, is not fully top-hardy in zones 5b to 6b, but is still useful as a border shrub or in masses. Erect clusters of white flowers appear in spring.

as a visual screen in informal landscapes. The name silky dogwood refers to the fine silky pubescence on twig tips and underneath young leaves, and it can be distinguished from red-osier dogwood at any season by its brown, rather than white, pith.

DIRCA PALUSTRIS (leatherwood), native to northern swamps, is seldom used as a landscape plant, yet offers unique seasonal interest, in addition to its tolerance of poorly drained and calcareous soils. A slow grower, this shrub can be counted on to remain below eye level for many years, retaining its compact shape without pruning. Small, tubular, pale yellow flowers open in early spring, shortly before the leaves start to unfold, and so are noticeable at close range. Leaves emerge pale green, changing to medium green as they expand fully to become elliptical and two to three

inches long. Stems are extremely pliable, giving the name "leatherwood", and have much the same appearance in winter as those of the deciduous daphnes, which are closely related.

FOTHERGILLA species (fothergillas) have received increasing attention in recent years, but still are not as widely used as would be expected from their garden and landscape assets. These shrubs are prime contenders for attention in the landscape in two seasons. In midspring, their upright bottlebrush-shaped clusters of creamy white flowers add delightful color during leaf unfolding—color that combines well with just about any other color. Yet autumn is this shrub's showiest season, as the neat, soft green, witch-hazellike leaves turn to brilliant gold overlaid with scarlet in "good" years, and soft gold to orange in quieter times. Dwarf fothergilla (*F. gardenii*) usually remains below three feet in height, slightly exceeding this eventually in shade, and has small flower clusters (just over an inch long), which become colorful before much leaf expansion has occurred. Flower clusters of large fothergilla (*F. major*) open a little later and are two to three inches long, in proportion to overall plant size. Large fothergilla is a magnificent shrub, useful for naturalizing, screening (but not quickly), or simply included in mixed shrub plantings for its distinctive landscape interest.

HYDRANGEA QUERCIFOLIA (oakleaf hydrangea), native from northern Alabama, Georgia, and Mississippi, to Florida, is surprisingly useful in the North as well. Even though it is not fully top-hardy in Zones 5b to 6b, it is still useful there as a massing or border shrub below eye level. In Zones 5 and 6 its flower buds survive mild winters. Even when the tops are winterkilled to the ground, the hardy rootstock sends up new shoots rapidly in the spring, forming a three-foot mound of foliage by late summer. The coarsely handsome leaves turn russet-red by midautumn. In the more southern areas where it is native, oakleaf hydrangea makes a shrub six to eight feet tall, and even broader, with the added appeal of great erect clusters of white flowers in spring.

HYPERICUM species (St. John's-worts) of shrubs reliably remain below three feet in height without pruning, thrive in full sun, tolerate considerable dryness, and make an impressive show of golden yellow flowers in midsummer. Three North American species: *H. frondosum* (golden St. John's-wort), *H. kalmianum* (Kalm St. John's-wort), and *H. prolificum* (shrubby St. John's-wort) are pretty much interchangeable in gardens and landscapes in Zones 5-9, and Kalm and shrubby St. John's-worts are useful northward at least to Zone 4b. Kalm St. John's-wort is the northernmost in origin, native from Quebec to Michigan. It has narrow leaves, only one to two inches long, and usually grows only two to three feet tall, with flowers less than an inch across. Shrubby St. John's-wort, native from New Jersey to Georgia, is slightly larger in all respects, growing to three feet tall. Golden St. John's-wort, native from the Carolinas to Texas, has blue-green leaves up to three inches long, and flowers close to two inches across. The popular selection, *H. frondosum* 'Sunburst', has performed very well for ten years at Purdue University (Zone 5b), including two extremely difficult winters (1983 and 1985), and has produced a good show of red-orange autumn foliage in most of those years.

ILEX GLABRA (inkberry) is native along the Atlantic and Gulf coastal plains from the Canadian Maritimes to Texas. With such a great natural range, it would be surprising if plants did not vary widely in cold hardiness, and perhaps heat tolerance as well. Forms adapted to extreme southern and northern climates may have been selected, but if so are not generally known about, and landscape use of this species is most common in the Mid-Atlantic region. This is a handsome evergreen growing eight to ten feet tall in good soil, but amenable to pruning for size control where necessary. A better solution, though, is to use one of the slower-growing cultivars such as 'Compacta', 'Densa', or 'Nordic', which may become tall eventually but will remain much lower for years. Leaves of inkberry are only an inch or two long, flat and lustrous, producing a "flatter" surface appearance than those of the Japanese holly (*Ilex crenata*) cultivars. Like all hollies, this one is dioecious, but since its black fruits add much less landscape interest than those of the red-fruited species, it makes no difference, in many applications, whether male or female plants are used. The selection 'Ivory Queen', however, has ivory-white fruits, with special winter interest, so the presence of a male plant in its vicinity for pollination becomes important.

MYRICA PENSYLVANICA (bayberry) must

have been one of the first sights the Pilgrims saw as they landed at Plymouth, since this shrub is so common on the North Atlantic seacoast from Nova Scotia to Maryland. Deciduous in the North and grading to at least semi-evergreen farther south, with two-inch leaves that are pleasantly aromatic when crushed, this handsome shrub is most useful as a massing plant, to be kept below eye level, when necessary, by pruning every five years or so. It can also be used as a specimen for accent or as a component of mixed-shrub plantings, for its unique foliage and fruiting interest. Female plants bear clusters of white-gray waxy fruits, which hang on the plant long after leaf-drop, and sometimes almost until spring. The heavy coating of wax that covers these fruits was extracted by boiling and used in candlemaking by early settlers, and this practice is still being carried out for the benefit of tourists who appreciate the bayberry aroma released as bayberry candles burn. Bayberry can convert atmospheric nitrogen to usable forms with the help of soil microorganisms, so it thrives in infertile soil, but it also grows well in the heavier, more fertile soils of most of the Midwest. As would be expected from its native habitat, it is unusually salt-tolerant, and tolerates dry soil as well, making it one of the most useful and troublefree North American shrubs, adaptable in Zones 5-9.

OEMLERIA CERASIFORMIS (Indian plum, formerly *Osmaronia*), is native to the coastal Pacific Northwest, and probably has its greatest landscape value there, although it might well be tried more fully in other regions. In *Gardening with Native Plants of the Pacific Northwest* (University of Washington Press, 1982), Arthur Kruckeberg points out that no other native shrub of the region "better celebrates the spring rebirth of our lowland landscapes." This shrub's small hanging clusters of white flowers, soon joined by the emerging pale green leaves, "light up the leafless woods" for several weeks in their native climate. Its

half-inch fruits are interesting at close range, colorful in their yellow-orange stage in early summer, and interesting as they ripen deep purple in late summer.

PIERIS FLORIBUNDA (mountain andromeda) is one of the hardiest and most beautiful of all broad-leaved evergreens. It is native to the mountains of the southeastern United States but adapted in landscape usage to much of the northeastern U.S. as well, and even the Midwest in sites having acidic, organic soils and protection from wind and full sun in winter. This is a lower, more moundlike plant than its more popular Japanese relative, *Pieris japonica*, and it seldom grows above eye level except in very shaded sites. It flowers a little later than Japanese andromeda, holding its flower clusters more erect, and its uniformly dark green, slightly rugose foliage offers pleasing texture. Most important of all for residents of northern areas is its winter hardiness, to Zone 5a, assuming good site selection and soil that is acidic (below pH 5.5) and well drained, but not excessively dry.

RHODODENDRON CANESCENS (Piedmont azalea), native from North Carolina to Florida and Texas, is the most spectacular of the pinxterbloom-type azaleas. It produces masses of fragrant white flowers with pink tubes opening in early spring, before and along with the new foliage. Its useful range extends northward at least into Zone 6b in the East. In more northern areas where it is not hardy it can be replaced by the equally fragrant roseshell azalea (*R. prinophyllum*) or the pinxterbloom (*R. periclymenoides*), which typically lacks fragrance. Where it is well adapted, though, Piedmont azalea is a clear first choice in this group.

RHODODENDRON VASEYI (pinkshell azalea) is one of the most distinctive of all azaleas. It is a native of North Carolina growing to ten feet tall in good sites. This shrub has almost clear pink flowers in great numbers in midspring. Two other features give this shrub special value: it thrives in fairly wet soil and it has some of the best foliage character to be found in the deciduous azaleas. Use in place of the hybrid azaleas, especially in naturalized and informal landscapes.

RHUS OVATA (sugarbush) is one of three entire-leaved sumacs from southern California—native to Arizona and Baja California as well. Sugarbush is a densely compact shrub growing from three or four feet tall and wide in desert sites to at least twice that size in semiarid climates. Its two- to three-inch leaves are evergreen, leathery and deep green with red margins when young, rounded with pointed tips. Clusters of small red dormant flower buds add interest at close range in winter, then open creamy white by late spring. Fuzzy red fruits develop, which in some years add color to female plants throughout the following winter. The lush green appearance of this shrub belies its tolerance of dry climates, and contrasts with its many silvery-gray companions on the desert. In spite of this lush look, sugarbush exhibits traits that suggest adaptation to dry climate: compact growth habit and thick, rounded leaves that cup downward, protecting the undersides of the leaves from wind. The closely related lemonade berry (*Rhus integrifolia*) differs only in minor ways, and is interchangeable in the dry southwestern landscapes where these shrubs are appropriately used.

SHEPHERDIA ROTUNDIFOLIA (roundleaf buffaloberry), unlike the more common species of *S. argentea* and *S. canadensis,* is evergreen, although it would be more descriptive to say ever-silver, since that is its color year-round. This shrub grows to three feet, and forms a compact mound of foliage. Few shrubs better illustrate morphological adaptation to dry climates. This compactness of foliage, the small, round, thick leaves, cupped downward, the dense mat of hairs on the lower leaf surfaces, and the reflective quality of the silvery scales that give the foliage its striking color, all conserve water in the plant. This shrub is not widely planted as yet, even in its native region, and its adaptability to other regions is largely untested. In arid climates, it offers striking visual appeal, and its spiny twig tips should make it useful as a physical barrier that will remain low enough to see over.

SOPHORA SECUNDIFLORA (Texas mountain laurel, mescal bean) is a tall evergreen shrub, sometimes to 25 feet and treelike. As a member of the Legume Family (Fabaceae) it is not at all closely related to the eastern mountain laurel (*Kalmia latifolia*), and of course neither plant belongs to the Laurel Family (Lauraceae). Mescal bean grows wild on limestone soils from central Texas to New Mexico and into Mexico, and is included in southwestern landscapes for its beautiful blue-violet flowers, borne in nodding clusters in early spring, as new foliage is unfolding. Their sweet fragrance is pleasant in minor amounts, but can be overwhelming for some people. The fuzzy brown constricted pods that follow are interesting, but add little to the plant's landscape value, and since the seeds are poisonous, some prefer to remove the pods before they mature. The dark green foliage, though, is an asset year-round. This shrub is perhaps best used as a specimen for accent, or to add early spring interest to mixed plantings. It is tall enough to serve as a visual screen, but not dense enough without frequent pruning.

VACCINIUM PARVIFOLIUM (red huckleberry) ranges widely as a native shrub in the coastal Pacific Northwest and on the lower western slopes of the Cascade Range and northern Sierra Nevada. Its flowers are barely noticeable, but the small bright red fruits that follow in early sumer add interest and are excellent in preserves and pies. The most significant landscape feature of this plant, though, is its foliage. The small, delicate leaves begin to unfold by mid-spring, and form lacy layers on the finely twigged branches. It retains its bright, pale green color throughout the unfolding process and for some time thereafter,

Rhododendron vaseyi

eventually turning to soft green, but never the dark green of so many of its companion species found in the Pacific Northwest in late summer. Nothing brightens a Douglas-fir forest like this shrub, caught in a ray of light penetrating the dark woodland.

VIBURNUM RUFIDULUM (southern black haw) is similar in many ways to the better known northern black haw (*Viburnum prunifolium*). It can be used as a large shrub or as a small patio tree. Both black haws are rather stiffly upright in their branching; both have excellent foliage with significant autumn color; and both become dense enough to make excellent hedges or informal visual screens. Southern black haw has more glossy, leathery foliage than its northern counterpart, and its fall foliage is magnificent—scarlet to mahogany leaves accentuated by highlights on the shiny leaves. Southern black haw is not as cold hardy as northern black haw, but plants have succeeded so far north of the native limits (southern Illinois to Virginia) that a cold-hardiness rating of Zone 6a seems conservative, and plants propagated from

those of northern origin probably will withstand most Zone 5 winters.

VIBURNUM TRILOBUM (American cranberry bush) is so similar to the more-often-planted European cranberry bush that some botanists have lumped them together as a single species. Yet there are a few differences. First, for native plant purists, American cranberry bush is indeed native across the North American continent, in the northern United States and most of adjacent Canada. Foliage of American cranberry bush is much more likely to color well in autumn than that of European cranberry bush. Timing of color is related to timing of acclimation in most shrubs, and so reflects on relative hardiness. But in this case, the difference in hardiness between the American and European cranberry bushes is of great concern only if you happen to live where average annual minimum temperatures are in the range of 40 to 50 degrees below zero. There, American cranberry bush clearly has the edge. Both cranberry bushes produce magnificent fruiting displays in autumn and well into winter, but the fruits of American cranberry bush are clearly preferred by makers of preserves.

All of these shrubs are functional landscape plants and all have distinctive visual character. They can be used in constructed landscapes in any appropriate sites within their native ranges, and many can be used far from home as well, since in virtually every case the useful range far exceeds the natural range. All can be used in traditionally designed landscapes or in restored plant communities, the ultimate in "natural landscaping" short of nature itself. The next step is to broaden this list for the region in which you live, and the ultimate challenge is to use your native shrubs well, whatever your design preference. 🍃

STRIKING NATIVES FOR THE PERENNIAL BORDER

EDITH R. EDDLEMAN

For sheer elegance in the spring garden, few plants can compete with the white wild indigo (*Baptisia lactea*).

When the term "herbaceous perennial" is used, many plants which spring to mind are native American plants: purple coneflower, blazing-stars, black-eyed Susans, Stokes' aster, New England aster (to name a few), but as one horticultural wit aptly observed, we Americans often fail to

EDITH R. EDDLEMAN *is curator and designer of the perennial border at North Carolina State University in Raleigh. The border features native and exotic perennial combinations. She is a garden designer, horticultural consultant and lecturer.*

notice the merits of our native plants until they have attended "finishing school" in English and European gardens. Sometimes easily propagated natives are not even available commercially in this country. For example, *Aster lateriflorus*, native from southeast Canada and Minnesota south to Florida, Missouri and Texas, whose tiny, white, autumn flowers have long been appreciated in English gardens, has only recently become available to U.S. gardeners (ironically from stock imported from

England and Germany). Perhaps the public is not entirely to blame for this lack of observance, for it is only in gardens where soil is prepared well, adequate water is supplied, plants are well-sited, and competition is quelled that the full potential of our natives can be appreciated.

It is often said native plants perform better simply because they are native and, hence, "better adapted," ignoring the diversity of geographic and climatic conditions in this country. Being native does not necessarily ensure that a plant will be more tolerant of drought, poor soil conditions or inadequate light. While knowledge of the plant's natural range and the conditions under which it grows gives a good indication of conditions which it can tolerate, this is not necessarily a complete indication of the plant's adaptability. An example of this is *Lobelia cardinalis*. Naturally occurring in wet areas of the central and eastern U.S., often in partially shaded sites, this plant can be grown beautifully in full sun and drier garden soils. Another example is *Penstemon smallii*, native to a narrow geographical range in the mountains of North Carolina and Tennessee. This Southerner is hardy at least as far north as Zone 5 (though its strict requirement for well-drained soil makes it short lived in the landscape). When thoughtfully chosen, native perennials often prove to be surprisingly adaptable and are beautiful in combination with each other and with "introduced" or exotic species.

Most important to designing a border is careful plant selection. The first question to ask is: Is the plant appropriate to the garden site and conditions? If, for example, you are faced with a soil which is constantly moist but exposed to the sun, then it is best to work with plants such as *Vernonia* spp., *Eupatorium* spp., *Hibiscus moscheutos, Aster novae-angliae, Aster novi-belgii, Lobelia cardinalis, Filipendula rubra, Boltonia* spp., and others which tolerate, but do not require, wet soils. Once plant-site compatibility is

achieved, the design elements of form, texture and color should be considered.

The shapes of plants provide the perennial border with a profile or cross-sectional form. The leaves and flower-bearing stems of these plants give geometric structure to the garden. Perennials generally have either vertical or horizontal growth habits but, for the purposes of design, it is useful to characterize their shapes as spiky, rounded (or oval), or creeping ("weavers").

Perennials with spiky leaves or flowering stems provide a strong vertical element in the garden. The leaves of *Yucca filamentosa* are a good example. When in bloom the tiered stalk of white bell-like flowers adds increased punctuation to the upright clump of evergreen foliage. Likewise, the stems of *Veronicastrum virginicum* rise to heights up to five feet, clothed in whorled dark green leaves topped by multibranched spires of small white flowers in mid summer. Other plants for vertical interest include the many species of *Liatris, Physostegia*, foliage of *Iris virginica* and many native grasses such as *Panicum virgatum*. Plants which offer vertical interest but whose flowers are not in spikes include *Filipendula rubra*, with fluffy, wide-spreading flower heads of tiny pink flowers borne on wiry stems above beautiful clumps of deep green foliage and *Eupatorium fistulosum* with imposing dome-shaped dusty-pink flower heads held 8-10 feet tall. *Baptisia* offers spikes of pea-shaped flowers in blue, white, cream or yellow (depending on the species) in mid- to late-spring; when out of flower, their large rounded clumps of foliage make a suitable background for other flowering perennials.

Other rounded forms are represented by *Amsonia, Boltonia asteroides*, many asters and *Euphorbia corollata* which, while rounded in form, also functions in the garden as a "weaver". Weavers are plants of creeping habit such as *Verbena canadensis* or plants with lax flowering stems such as *Campanula rotundifolia* which creep through their garden companions without overpowering them. These can easily be distinguished from such beautiful "thugs" as *Oenothera speciosa* whose creeping root-stocks are capable of doing battle and winning against such well-known invaders as the non-clumping forms of *Artemisia*. In addition to their blending qualities, many creeping plants offer a textural contrast to the leaves and flowers through which they weave.

Texture is an important consideration in perennial garden design. Plants with fine textures—small, airy sprays of flowers or narrow leaves—recede visually. Coarse textures hold the eye. *Hibiscus moscheutos*, with its large leaves and flowers is a good example of an eye-catcher. Changes in texture provide focal points in the border. For example, the bold golden daisies of *Rudbeckia fulgida* contrast with the delicate white flower sprays of *Artemisia lactiflora**. Adding another visual layer of texture to the garden are the airy "see-through" plants, such *Verbena hastata*, taller species of *Aquilegia* such as *A. canadensis* with red and yellow flowers or *A. chrysanthus* with yellow flowers, and *Gaura lindheimeri*, which soften hard edges and provide a sense of depth to the garden.

Color, like texture, can affect our perception of visual space and provide a focal point in the garden. Warm colors (red, yellow, orange) shoot forward, shortening space. The use of large numbers of these warm-color flowered plants in a garden can make it appear smaller. Red, yellow and orange flowers and foliage colors are attention-getting, providing intense natural focal points in the border. Native plants with red flowers include *Lobelia cardinalis* and *Silene virginica*; yellows are represented by the many *Solidago* species and *Helianthus* species. Natives with true orange flowers are less common, but *Asclepias tuberosa* and *Lilium superbum* are examples.

Cool-colored flowers and foliage (blue, purple, green) recede from the eye and are more restful and soothing. The use of these colors can create a sense of distance and give a soft, misty quality to the garden. Good choices of blue-flowered natives are amsonias, scutellarias, *Lobelia siphilitica* and *Phlox divaricata*. *Verbena, Vernonia, Liatris,* and *Aster* species provide many shades of red-violet or purple. Green, the most prevalent color in nature, is provided in a variety of shades and tints by the foliage of herbaceous perennials, trees and shrubs.

White- and silver-foliaged plants intensify our perception of the colors associated with them. Hence, the red flowers of *Lobelia cardinalis* look brighter when viewed against the white flowers of *Boltonia asteroides* than when seen against the more closely related color hue of the golden yellow flowers of *Rudbeckia*. Placing complementary colors side-by-side (red-green, blue-orange, yellow-violet/purple) also intensifies the color effect and forces the eye to pause and refocus, creating natural focal points. The use of closely related colors in association with each other, however, creates a color harmony which allows the eye to pass over it and is more restful, (for example, red, yellow and orange flowers used together or pink and lavender flowers used together.)

Bloom colors are not the only color factor in the perennial garden. Silver-foliaged plants such as *Artemisia stelleriana* and blue-foliaged plants like *Eryngium yuccifolium* have a brightening effect as do white flowers and complementary colors. Conversely, bronze, deep purple or brown-tinged foliage such as the chocolate-brown foliage of *Lysimachia ciliata* and purple-tinged leaves of *Viola labradorica* have a calming effect upon the colors adjacent to them in the garden.

The vast flora of the continental U.S. offers the thoughtful gardener almost unlimited choices of plants for the border, each of which can fulfill one or more of the design functions described above. The choices outlined below represent a few examples of fine native plants from which we can choose; many have a wide geographic range and are adaptable to all areas of the continental U.S. Others have a narrow range of distribution but have proven hardy and dependable both north and south of that range.

For sheer elegance in the spring garden, few plants can compete with a mature clump of **Baptisia lactea** (synonym *B. pendula*), the white wild indigo. In spring many succulent-looking charcoal-gray stems emerge from the earth; reaching a height of three feet, they are soon clothed in dark gray-tinged green leaves. Above the foliage are spikes of creamy white flowers which are a striking contrast to the gray stems. The flowers open over a period of two weeks. Growing in dry open woods and clearings from Florida north to North Carolina, *B. lactea* grows best in well-drained soils and is hardy to Zone 6. When grown in full sun in moderately fertile soil, it will produce many flower spikes and form a dense moundlike clump of foliage which creates an excellent background and contrast to other later-flowering perennials. Gardeners north of Zone 6 can substitute the equally beautiful northern species *Baptisia leucantha* growing to four feet tall with a natural range from Minnesota south to Texas. (Botanists now lump this with *B. lactea* although horticulturally there are distinctions.) The white spikes of *Baptisia* make a nice contrast with the rounded forms of shrub roses and with the rounded flowers and vertical foliage of Siberian iris in the spring border.

Deserving of more notice is **Scutellaria incana**, the greater skullcap. Growing two to four feet tall, this beautiful perennial offers the gardener three-quarter inch, slightly fuzzy gray-blue flowers borne in spires from mid-summer to frost. If the foliage is cut back by half in early June, many more flower spikes will be produced, and the plant can be maintained at a height of two and one-half to three feet. A very hardy plant, it grows from Canada south to Virginia and west to Missouri. In the garden its soft blue flowers are especially beautiful in late summer if planted next to white flowers such as *Boltonia asteroides* or a large silver-leaved mound of *Artemisia* 'Silver King'. It is an especially good contrast in early fall to pink-flowered forms of *Aster novae-angliae* and with violet-colored, late-fall-blooming *Aster grandiflorus*. In July, a soft and misty effect can be obtained by interplanting clumps of *Scutellaria incana* with the lacy white flowers of *Daucus carota* (Queen Anne's lace).*

Welcome at the end of summer are the red-violet flowers of **Liatris aspera.** Growing six feet tall, three-quarters of the stem is covered in compact bracted flower buds which appear to be carved from ivory and pale green jade. Even before it flowers, *L. aspera* offers a sculptural quality to the garden which shows off noticeably against a dark green background such as an evergreen hedge. All the bracts turn a red-violet just prior to the emergence of red-violet threadlike flowers. The fully open flowers resemble one-and-a-half-inch fringed buttons. The flower spikes are so heavy that staking may be required; a single tall stake per stem works best. The flowers combine well with pink-flowered asters or *Boltonia* and contrast beautifully with *Rudbeckia triloba*, a dainty black-eyed Susan blooming from late summer through frost with flowers standing from warm golden-yellow near the black eye to butter-yellow at the tips of the petals. For a truly smashing effect, combine *L. aspera* with the airy pure-yellow Queen-Anne's-lace-like flowers of *Patrinia scabiosifolia** (three to seven feet tall) backed by the striking horizontally yellow-banded foliage of *Miscanthus sinensis* 'Strictus'.* *L. aspera* grows in well-drained soils from Ontario south to Texas and South Carolina. For gardeners with damp soil, *Liatris spicata*, a southern wetlands species hardy at least to Zone 3, would work equally well in the garden.

60

A dainty *Liatris* look-alike is **Carphephorus paniculatus** (formerly *Trilisia paniculatus*), native to damp areas of the Southeast coastal plain but adaptable to drier soils. It is hardy to Zone 6, growing 12 to 24 inches tall in sunny locations. In early fall single spikes of soft red-violet flowers emerge from dense grasslike clumps of foliage. It can be planted with *Chrysopsis mariana*, a dryland species whose clusters of bright yellow flowers bloom at the same time as *Carphephorus*. A larger species of *C. odoratissimus* grows to three to four feet and is more cold hardy.

The southern perennial border is brightened in April by the pale, steely-blue flower clusters of **Amsonia ciliata**. This native of the southeastern U.S. grows in the sandhills and in open sandy woodlands. Mature plants form dense clumps of stems clothed in narrow, dark-green leaves which add a fine texture to the garden. *A. ciliata* grows best in full sun and well drained soil. In the spring garden, its blue flowers and fine foliage contrast beautifully with the yellow and green marbled foliage of *Sedum erythrostictum** 'Mediopictum', yellow-flowered *Aquilegia canadensis* 'Corbett' and the deeper blue flowers of *Sisyrinchium atlanticum* while the soft blue flower heads of *Phlox divaricata* repeat the blue of the *Amsonia* flowers.

Another choice native for the spring border is **Phlox pilosa**. Given a sunny or semishaded location, this 18-inch-tall phlox bears fragrant clusters of white-eyed, mauve-pink flowers for two-and-one-half months. A wide ranging species, it occurs from southeastern Connecticut to southern Florida, west to Wisconsin and south to Texas. In the garden it combines well with the large fringed lavender-blue flowers of *Stokesia laevis* and spiky veronicas; it is even more pleasing when combined with the pale red-violet flower spikes of *Penstemon smallii*.

PENSTEMON SMALLII grows 18 to 24 inches tall and bears spikes of flowers above dark

Phlox pilosa ozarkana is an 18-inch tall phlox that bears fragrant clusters of white-eyed, mauve-pink flowers for two and one half months.

green, red-backed foliage in late spring. If the old stalks are cut back, it will continue to produce new spikes through the summer. Occurring in a very limited range in lightly shaded woodlands and open banks in the mountains of North Carolina and Tennessee, it is surprisingly cold hardy (at least Zone 5). While flexible as to its light requirements, it requires sharp drainage and tends to be a short-lived perennial, requiring frequent division. It is easily grown from seed. In the garden, it combines well with the large yellow cup-shaped flowers of *Oenothera missouriensis* or the tall flat yellow flower heads of *Achillea* 'Moonshine'* and *Chrysogonum virginianum*.

Hundreds of one inch white daisylike flowers cover six-feet-tall plants of **BOLTONIA ASTEROIDES** during August and September. Native to damp areas of the central and southeastern U.S., *B. asteroides* adapts easily to dry soils and flowers best in full sun.

Prior to its bloom, the shiny silver-green foliage is an excellent foil for earlier blooming perennials such as *Echinacea purpurea*. A shorter selection of *B. asteroides*, 'Snowbank', grows to four feet. Combine the rounded form of *B. asteroides* with either of two blue salvias native to Texas, *Salvia azurea* var. *grandiflora* or *Salvia farinacea* and clumps of *Sedum* 'Autumn Joy'* for a pleasing late summer/early fall garden picture.

A soft pink-flowered form of *B. asteroides*, 'Pink Beauty', grows four feet tall. Plant it in combination with the shrubby *Lespedeza thunbergii**, whose drooping racemes of deep red-violet, pea-shaped flowers are a pleasing contrast to the rounded flowers and form of this *Boltonia*. The pink flower spikes of *Physostegia virginiana* contrast in form with both the *Boltonia* and *Lespedeza;* the colors of their flowers create a pleasing color harmony. Both *B. asteroides* and *P. virginiana* grow in wet soils but adapt to average to dry garden conditions.

Equally beautiful with *B. asteroides* is **Vernonia noveboracensis**, rising to a height of eight feet, depending on available soil moisture. Naturally occurring in wet meadows, stream banks, and roadside ditches throughout the eastern U.S., it bears dense clusters of tufted, deep violet flowers from July to September. Its tall, rounded form combines well with pink-flowered forms of *Aster novae-angliae* and the feathery pink-tinged flower panicles of *Eragrostis trichodes*.

ERAGROSTIS TRICHODES is native from Illinois west to Colorado and south to Texas. It grows four to five feet tall and flowers from July to September; it tends to be floppy and should be grown through a wire hoop to prevent it from smothering smaller plants located nearby.

Flowering for three to four weeks in early fall, **SOLIDAGO RUGOSA** grows four feet tall. This native of eastern woods, meadows, fields, bogs and pine barrens is as adaptable in the garden as it is in its natural range, tolerating either wet or dry soils.

The many fine-textured, arching, single-sided panicles of small yellow flowers complement fall-flowering asters such as *Aster novae-angliae* and *A. pilosus*. Combine it with *Liatris aspera*, or the shorter *L. graminifolia*, or *Boltonia asteroides* for an elegant look, or contrast its rounded form with the flower spikes of *Lobelia siphilitica* or *Scutellaria incana*.

An unusual member of the aster family, **ASTER CONCOLOR** has upright stems two and one-half feet tall clothed in opposite, silky, gray-green leaves which are held vertically against the stems. At each leaf node is a single flower bud. In September, as these buds swell and begin to open, the stems arch gracefully in a cascade of deep violet-blue flowers. The flowers show off against the light gray-green foliage of wooly thymes and are equally beautiful spilling through the fluffy white clouds of *Euphorbia corollata*.

Often despised for its aggressive habits in the deep rich soils of the Midwest, **EUPHORBIA COROLLATA** can be a well-mannered and useful addition to the perennial border. Growing from Ontario south to Florida and Texas, this member of the spurge family will grow in almost any garden. It may take up to three years for the creeping rootstock to become thoroughly established and for the stems to reach three feet in height. The lax stems weave easily among other flowers or can fill gaps left by summer-dormant plants such as oriental poppies. The small greenish flowers are produced in summer months and are surrounded by long-lasting white petallike structures which give the plant its frothy appearance. *E. corollata* combines well with *Gaillardia* and *Rudbeckia fulgida* and is elegant in combination with blue salvias, *Platycodon grandiflorus** (balloon flowers) and silver-foliaged plants.

Two very different verbenas for the border are the tall **VERBENA HASTATA** and *V. CANADENSIS* (rose verbena). *V. hastata* forms clumps with stems three to four feet tall clothed in green-toothed leaves ending in a green upright spike around which appear tiny lavender-blue flowers. This verbena flowers from late May till frost with the flower spike elongating all the while. Its effect in the landscape resembles a soft blue mist and, despite it height, it is an excellent addition to the front of the border, softening the view of the plants behind it. It is tough enough to combine with such aggressive 'thugs' as the beautiful white-flowered *Lysimachia clethroides** (goose-neck loosestrife). Add to this combination clumps of *Platycodon grandiflorus,** whose fat blue flower buds give rise to its common name, balloon flower, for a long-flowering midsummer combination.

Verbena canadensis is hardly to Zone 5 and is grown as an annual farther north. Its range includes the eastern seaboard from Virginia south, west to Iowa and Colorado and south into Mexico. In the South it bears clusters of fragrant flowers ranging from deep purple, dark and light lavender to pink, from early March to frost. In the milder parts of its range, its foliage turns a pleasing purple in winter, while in colder climates it may die back to the ground. In the garden this verbena seems to require dividing and soil replenishment every two years to assure the best bloom. For a spring effect, combine *V. canadensis* with P*hlox pilosus, Aquilegia* and *Iris tectorum**. Later in the year its rich purple flowers are an excellent complement to the golden flowers of *Rudbeckia fulgida* 'Goldsturm.'

Another little-known native, whose sprawling stems make it appear to be of creeping habit, is perennial blue day flower, **COMMELINA ERECTA**, whose habit belies its name. Unlike its larger, weedy, introduced, annual cousin, *C. communis*, it is a fine addition to the border. Its ruffled petaled flowers are larger and of a softer blue than the annual species and are produced over a long period from midsummer through early fall (though each flower lasts but a single day). It grows from New York to Florida and west to Texas. Allow the stems of *C. erecta* to clamber around the gray-blue lance-shaped leaves of *Eryngium yuccifolium* and back up both with the soft yellow flowers of *Coreopsis verticillata* 'Moonbeam'.

Among the longest-blooming of plants for the border is **GAURA LINDHEIMERI**. It begins to flower in May while only 12 inches tall. Throughout its long season of bloom, the flowering stems continue to elongate, reaching six feet before frost finishes the last of its flowers. Seen from a distance, the plants have many stems bearing airy white flowers; on close examination the flower buds are tinged with red, and the old flower buds fade to a soft salmon-pink above green and red mottled stems. Fresh flowers are produced daily. *Gaura* grows on well-drained soils from Louisiana south to Texas and into Mexico; it is hardy as far north as Zone 6. It is important to site this plant carefully in the garden, for it produces a large woody taproot and resents disturbances. It is very tolerant of heat and drought. Grow it in the center of the border or near the front to take advantage of its see-through quality. Grown in front of a dark-flowered, dark-foliaged *Buddleia** such as 'Purple Prince', it is striking as it is rising from a mass of other white-flowered and silver-foliaged plants such as the white-flowered form of *Verbena tenuisecta**, *Euphorbia corollata*, and silver-foliaged *Artemisia* 'Powis Castle'*.

The plants mentioned above are only a small sampling of choice natives available for use in the perennial border so investigate the flowers of your region, and check the listings of the increasing number of nurseries which propagate natives for other ideas and suggestions. 🌿

See Table on next page for the common names and USDA hardiness zones of all the native plants mentioned in this article.

*Editor's Note: These plants are not U.S. natives.

T A B L E 1

SUMMARY OF NATIVE PLANTS MENTIONED.
Plants in boldface are featured in the article.

Scientific Name	Common Name	USDA Hardiness Zone	Scientific Name	Common Name	USDA Hardiness Zone
Amsonia ciliata	**blue star**	6	Iris virginica	southern blue flag	
Aquilegia canadensis 'Corbett'	columbine	2-8	**Liatris aspera**	**button snakeroot**	**3-9**
			Liatris graminifolia	blazing star	6-9
Aquilegia chrysanthus	columbine	4-8	Liatris spicata	blazing star	3-9
Artemisia stelleriana	beach wormwood	2-9	Lilium superbum	Turk's cap lily	5-8
Asclepias tuberosa	butterfly weed	3-9	Lobelia cardinalis	cardinal flower	2-8
Aster concolor	**eastern silvery aster**	**5-9**	Lobelia siphilitica	great blue lobelia	4-8
Aster grandiflorus	large flowered aster	7-9	Lysimachia ciliata		2-8
Aster lateriflorus	calico aster	3-9	Oenothera missouriensis	Missouri evening primrose	3-9
Aster novae-angeliae	New England aster	3-8			
Aster novi-belgii	New York aster		Oenothera speciosa	Mexican evening primrose	5-9
Aster pilosus	frost aster				
Baptisia lactea	**white wild indigo**	6	Panicum virgatum	switchgrass	3-10
Boltonia asteroides 'Pink Beauty' 'Snowbank'	**thousand-flower aster**	4-9	**Penstemon smallii**	**Small's beardtongue**	**5-7**
			Phlox divaricata	wild sweet William	3-8
Campanula rotundifolia	bluebells	2-8	**Phlox pilosa**	**downy phlox**	**3-10**
Carphephorus odoratissimus		6	Physostegia virginiana	obedient plant	3-9
Carphephorus paniculatus		6	Rudbeckia fulgida 'Goldsturm'	black-eyed Susan	4-9
Chrysogonum virginianum	green-and-gold	4-9	**Rudbeckia triloba**	**black-eyed Susan**	**5-8**
Chrysopsis mariana	Maryland golden-aster	5-8	Salvia farinacea	mealycup sage	7-9
Commelina erecta	**blue day flower**	4	Salvia azurea var. grandiflora	blue salvia	5-9
Coreopsis verticillata 'Moonbeam'	whorled tickseed	3-9	**Scutellaria incana**	**greater skullcap**	**2-6**
Echinacea purpurea	purple coneflower		Silene virginica	fire-pink	3-8
Eragrostis trichodes	**sand love grass**		Sisyrinchium atlanticum	blue-eyed grass	3-9
Eryngium yuccifolium	rattlesnake master	3-9	**Solidago rugosa**	**rough leaved goldenrod**	**4-9**
Eupatorium fistulosum	Joe-Pye weed	4-9	Stokesia laevis	Stokes' aster	6-9
Euphorbia corollata	**prairie-baby's breath**	**3-9**	**Verbena hastata**	**simpler's joy**	**3-9**
Filipendula rubra	queen-of-the-prairie	3-9	**Verbena canadensis**	**rose verbena**	**6**
Gaillardia	blanket flower	7-9	**Vernonia noveboracensis**	**ironweed**	**5-8**
Gaura lindheimeri		**5-10**	Vernonicastrum virginicum	Culver's root	3-9
Hibiscus moscheutos	marsh mallow	5-9	Viola labradorica	Labrador violet	2-8

NATIVE PLANTS AS GROUND COVERS

SUGGESTIONS FROM A CONNECTICUT GARDENER

JUDY GLATTSTEIN

As any gardener knows, bare ground is an invitation for weeds to grow. If you do not mulch or plant, something will appear to occupy the open space. Use of plants as ground cover fills the space, and the plants serve to unify the garden. In addition, a drift or sweep of a single plant is visually pleasing. But not all plants are equally suited to function as ground cover.

Consider the dogtooth violet, *Erythronium americanum*. The handsome mottled leaves appear early in spring. But this plant

JUDY GLATTSTEIN *is a landscape consultant working with native plants in naturalistic designs. She has taught wildflower cultivation and propagation courses for The New York Botanical Garden and The New England Wild Flower Society. A freelance writer/photographer, her work has appeared in many national magazines. She was guest editor of* **Plants & Gardens** *handbook* **Plants for Problem Places***.*

goes dormant by late May or early June. This means that the ground is bare throughout much of the growing season. Any of the spring ephemerals, those plants which flower early and then go dormant, are a poor choice for this purpose.

What then, are the parameters we should use? A ground-cover plant should have neat attractive foliage. If the leaves are evergreen then the plant will also be interesting in late fall and winter. Flowers are a bonus, but are too short-term to be the definitive criterion. The plants should be spreading. Then fewer plants are required in the beginning. It is rare that a plant will meet all the above suggestions. They serve as a means of comparing one plant to another, and making a decision as to which will be selected for use as a ground cover.

In the wild, plants grow in a particular

area, referred to as their range. Certainly they can be expected to grow in other areas with similar conditions of soil and climate. Often, these plants will be genetically adaptable to somewhat different conditions as well. Plants from the Piedmont can grow in New England. Use the original range to start with and experiment from there.

One excellent choice is a woodland phlox, **Phlox stolonifera**. It has neat evergreen foliage only a couple of inches high. The plants spread by surface runners which root down at the nodes. Flowers appear in May, carried well above the leaves. Color is typically a soft blue. Cultivars exist which provide the native plant enthusiast with lavender ('Sherwood's Purple'), pink ('Sherwood's Pink') or white ('Bruce's White') forms. This plant is easily propagated and relatively common in the nursery trade. *P. stolonifera* is found from Pennsylvania and Ohio south to South Carolina and Georgia.

Another favorite of mine is a non-flowering plant. This is the Christmas fern, **Polystichum acrostichoides**. The lacy evergreen fronds provide winter interest. In the spring the new fronds, covered with chaffy brown scales, uncoil and unroll. The new fronds stand erect and graceful through the summer. Then in autumn they begin to arch over and assume a more horizontal habit. This fern does not run and spread; it does make ever-increasing clumps which can be lifted and divided to provide additional plants. This adaptable fern is found in the wild from Nova Scotia to southeastern Wisconsin, south to central Florida and eastern Texas.

The glossy green leaves of the Japanese pachysandra make it a popular component for many shady landscapes. This common species happens to have an American cousin. This is the Allegheny spurge, **Pachysandra procumbens** with softer, duller green foliage. Mature leaves exhibit a lovely mottling. This plant is evergreen in my garden (Zone 6), but is reported to be deciduous in more severe climates. Flowers are attractive fuzzy spikes like a white bottle-brush, in the spring.

P. procumbens is easy to propagate by cuttings taken in June. Use a gritty mix of equal parts sand and peat moss. Pack lightly into cell packs (those 6-compartmented units many annuals are sold in). Water well, then drain. Take the cuttings, wound each lightly down one side with your thumb nail. Dip in rooting hormone. Set the cuttings one to a compartment. Make arched supports from wire coat hangers. Cover a tray-full of six-packs with a clear plastic bag supported on the wire hoops so that is doesn't touch the cuttings. Set the "covered wagon" in a lightly shaded site out of direct sunlight. In a few weeks roots will form. This is an easy way to propagate many plants from cuttings. Our native pachysandra is found from Kentucky to Florida and Louisiana.

Mayapple, **Podophyllum peltatum**, is a quickly spreading plant suitable for large areas. It is deciduous. Given a shady site with moist soil the leaves will remain in good condition through summer. Often the leaves will begin to yellow and go dormant in mid-summer if the soil is dry. The white flowers nod, and are hidden beneath the leaves. They are followed by attractive fruits which are not edible. May-apple is found from Florida to Texas, north to Minnesota and Ontario.

Another good shade-tolerant ground cover is **Vancouveria hexandra.** Called American barrenwort, this plant is reminiscent of epimedium, another Japanese import. The dainty foliage is made up of three oval leaflets. The delicate appearance disguises an iron constitution. Given the humus-rich soil and woodland shade it needs, the plant is very long-lived and vigorous. Small white flowers in the spring are an extra bonus. A northwest native, **Vancouveria** grows wild in Washington, Oregon and northern California.

Foamflower, **Tiarella cordifolia,** has

masses of small white flowers on a slender stem about eight inches tall in the spring. The leaves are dense and form a good cover in moderate shade. Spreading by surface or just-below-surface runners, foamflower will make a large colony. It is helpful if the colony is given a top-dressing (light sprinkling) of compost in early spring. Do not use fertilizer as the plant is easily "burned" and damaged foliage will result. Foamflower is native from Ontario south to Georgia and Alabama.

A small shrub which is useful as a ground cover is pachystima, **Paxistima canbyi**. Growing about one foot high, this shrub does well in sun or light to medium shade with a sandy, peaty soil. The narrow evergreen leaves are slightly toothed near the tips. Grown where they receive some sun the leaves often turn an attractive bronze color in the fall. Flowers are inconspicuous. *Paxistima* is found on Appalachian mountain tops in Virginia and West Virginia.

Another good choice for sun or light shade is green-and-gold, **Chrysogonum virginianum** var. **australe**. This is the very low-growing form of the species. The dark green leaves make a dense mat. Small bright yellow daisy flowers make a good display in the spring and some repeat bloom in areas with cooler summers. In northern areas snow cover is important for winter survival. Green-and-gold is native from Pennsylvania and West Virginia to Florida and Louisiana.

In very sandy soil areas with full sun nothing is better than our native juniper, **Juniperus horizontalis**. This standby of the nursery trade is available in several horticultural selections such as 'Bar Harbor' and 'Wiltonii' (also known as 'Blue Rug'). The needlelike foliage is a silvery-blue in the named forms, often turning to a purple-bronze in winter. Female plants have glaucous blue berries. *Juniperus horizontalis* has a native range from Nova Scotia to Alaska, south to New Jersey, Minnesota and Montana. Another useful species is **Juniperus communis** which is found in northern parts of Asia and Europe as well as North America. 'Gold Beach' is a creeping form with bright yellow-green needles which makes a dense, matlike ground cover. It is a selection from the Pacific Northwest.

Bear-berry, **Arctostaphylos uva-ursi**, is good for full sun and a sandy peaty soil, but can be difficult to establish. Wintergreen, **Gaultheria procumbens**, is a charming evergreen woody plant for a humus-rich acid soil in part shade. It does not make a dense cover without a lot of attention to top-dressing and mulching. Galax, **Galax urceolata**, is a clump-forming evergreen plant with circular tooth-edged leaves which turn red-bronze in the fall. Minute white flowers are clustered on a long slender stalk. The clumps expand slowly and deer adore it. (Beware, this is a plant frequently dug from the wild and offered for sale.)

Wherever you intend to use ground-cover plants, site preparation is very important. Dig over the entire area to be planted, removing competing weeds and roots. Add soil amendments such as compost as necessary. Set the plants with spacing adjusted for their growth habits—Mayapple further apart than Christmas fern for example. Water the plants well and mulch. Shredded leaves or rough compost or pinebark mulch are especially suitable in a woodland setting. The latter or gravel would be good in sunny sites. Pay attention to watering the first season, especially during summer drought. Watch, and remove any weeds that may grow the first season. Going into winter make sure that woody plants in particular are well-watered. If snow cover is limited, consider protecting new plantings with evergreen boughs or salt hay.

The use of ground covers to unify the garden scene, to display a specimen plant, to reduce maintenance, are all as valuable in a native plant garden as in any other type of landscape. 🐦

Indian grass, *Sorghastrum nutans*, is near the top of the list of all garden grasses. 'Sioux Blue', a vegetatively propagated cultivar, has foliage of the softest powder blue. Photo by Rick Darke

NATIVE AMERICAN GRASSES

SUPERB LATE-SEASON
PERENNIALS FOR THE GARDEN

RICK DARKE

L ike ferns, perennial grasses are often overlooked when considering plants for the wild garden, yet much of the beauty of natural "gardens" across the landscape of wild America is due to the presence of our native grasses.

Grasses uniquely contribute a fine-textured, mostly vertical line, providing stunning contrast to broad-leaved companions. Sunlight plays wondrously through the narrow foliage, creating myriad changing patterns. Although individually minute, the flowers of many grasses are borne in profuse, upright clusters, their translucent parts glowing like candles in the setting sun. Grasses sway sensuously with the gentlest breeze, bringing movement and a delightful spontaneity into the gardened landscape.

Although most true grasses (members of the grass family, Gramineae) prefer sunny sites, they are otherwise very adaptable to a wide range of soil, temperature and moisture conditions, and are relatively disease-free.

Maintenance generally consists of cutting-back old growth once a year and

RICK DARKE'S *work as Longwood Gardens' curator of plants has taken him around the world in search of new plants for American gardens. His special interests include native American plants and ornamental grasses, both native and exotic. His home garden in Pennsylvania features wildflowers and grasses.*

occasional lifting and dividing of clumps. Seed propagation is easy in most cases although selected forms such as those having particular foliage colors are best propagated by division.

Grasses are particularly suited to wildflower gardens since they reach their peak during late summer and fall, a time when many more typical wildflowers, especially the spring ephemerals, are at low ebb. Summer foliage colors from lush greens to bright blue are often followed by autumn orange, red and gold. Flower tints range from silver to bronze. Many grasses are effective long after the growing season, and their winter hues of chestnut, almond, russet and fawn are excellent companions to brightly colored shrubs such as the red winterberry holly, *Ilex verticillata*. Here are some of the most interesting and reliable performers.

Many of the finest native grasses for gardens trace their origins to our once-vast tallgrass prairies and great plains, long since replaced by amber waves of exotic grain. The full range of native prairie species extends over much of the U.S., and includes some of our cold-hardiest grasses. Although requiring full sun, most are very drought-tolerant. Big bluestem, **Andropogon gerardii**, a clump-forming giant, grows four to eight feet tall and in August produces three-parted flower heads resembling turkey's feet. The foliage turns from rich green to copper-red in fall. Little bluestem, **Schizachyrium scoparium**, formerly *Andropogon scoparius* is common in prairie remnants and dry hills over much of the eastern U.S. Usually under three feet in height, its dense clumps of fine-textured foliage are delightful in mass. Summer leaves vary from bright green to aqua blue, and autumn colors include every shade of copper, red and bronze. Along the upper part of each stem, silky-white seedheads glow in the sunlight from October through to the following spring. Cultivar 'Aldous' has glaucous blue leaves. Close relative broom sedge, **Andropogon virginicus**, is not particularly associated with the prairie, but is native on open ground, sterile hills and sandy soil over much of North America. It is similar to but slightly coarser than little bluestem, and has many variant forms of garden interest.

An 18-inch fountain of the finest textured leaves springs from each clump of prairie dropseed, **Sporobolus heterolepis**. Topped by delicately open panicles of flowers in early August, the foliage turns pumpkin-orange in time for Halloween.

Indian grass, **Sorghastrum nutans**, is near the top of the list of all the garden grasses. A once constant companion to big bluestem in the tallgrass prairie, it is still found native in nearly every state from Arizona east. Strictly vertical in habit, it is variable in stature and foliage color. Indian grass can top six feet in the prairie but is more commonly four feet tall in the east. The medium-textured foliage is usually a deep green, but glaucous forms are frequent in prairie strains. 'Sioux Blue', a vegetatively propagated cultivar, has foliage of the softest powder blue. Indian grass produces golden-bronze terminal flower clusters beginning in late August. Hundreds of conspicuously bright yellow pollen sacs dangle on short threads from each cluster, tying in well with a lemon-flowered *Coreopsis verticillata* 'Moonbeam'

that might be planted nearby. Fall color is a golden-orange.

In eastern meadows, Indian grass is often accompanied by purpletop, **Tridens flavus.** Flowering two to three feet tall from August to September, purpletop can truly put a purple top on sunny meadows, and is magnificent when it occurs in huge sweeps alternating with the golden-bronze of Indian grass.

Its flower stalks reaching seven feet in height, prairie cord grass, **Spartina pectinata**, once covered hundreds of square miles in bottomlands too moist for other prairie grasses. Well adapted to average garden moisture, it spreads somewhat rapidly by rhizomes. Cultivar 'Aureomarginata' is a selected garden form with bright yellow leaf margins.

In nature, the tall prairie grasses were often accompanied by bold, broad-leaved plants including prairie dock *Silphium terebinthinacium*, compass plant *S. laciniatum*, and purple coneflowers *Echinacea purpurea* and *E. pallida*. Such plants make excellent garden companions to the grasses, providing a dramatic interplay of contrasting textures.

The Great Plains are drier than the tallgrass prairie, and grasses there are typically shorter-growing types. Two garden-worthy plains species belong to the genus **Bouteloua**. At 12 inches tall, blue grama, also called mosquito grass, **B. gracilis**, is among the shortest of our native ornamentals. Its curious flowers, beginning in June, are arranged like tiny brushes suspended horizontally from the tip of each stem. It is best in a sunny garden spot near a path or atop a ledge, where its detail can be closely appreciated. Side-oats grama, **Bouteloua curtipendula**, is a useful medium-sized species suitable for mass planting. Starting in July, ruler-straight flowering stalks radiate from the relatively low-mounded foliage. Individual flower clusters are attached at an angle along one side of each stalk and are purple at first appearance, bleaching to sand. Additional stalks are produced through the rest of the growing season until a complete arc is formed. Side-oats grama is native over much of the central U.S.

The range of many grasses extends beyond North America to Europe and Asia. A familiar garden plant, the blue-leaved sheep fescue, **Festuca ovina var. glauca**, grows natively in sunny open woods and stony slopes in our northwestern states, but is also widespread in Eurasia. Reed canary grass, **Phalaris arundinacea**, is native to river banks and other moist, sunny places in most of our northern states, and is also a Eurasian native. Known as gardener's garters or ribbon grass, a form with boldly white-variegated foliage, *P. arundinacea picta* has been a popular garden plant for over a century. Wood millet, **Milium effusum**, is native to both the northeastern U.S. and Eurasia. Cultivar 'Aureus' is valued for its bright charteuse leaves in early spring, which later darken to green. Another American-Eurasian native, tufted hair grass, **Deschampsia caespitosa**, is useful for its evergreen basal foliage and fine-textured flowering effect. The striking gray-blue leaves of American dune grass, which is now considered to be of the same species as the European blue lyme grass, **Elymus arenarius**, offer the opportunity for exciting combinations with summer flowers.

Switch grass, **Panicum virgatum**, grows three to five feet tall in a variety of dry to moist habitats in nearly all states from Nevada east. Upright in habit, it produces masses of finely branched flower clusters by mid-August. In typical forms, the green leaves turn gold in autumn although selection 'Heavy Metal' offers steel-blue summer foliage, and the foliage of 'Hanse-Herms' turns deep burgundy-red in fall. Both are propagated by division. The unusually wide leaves of relative *Panicum clandestinum* (or *Dichanthelium clandestinum*, as this has recently been classified), deer-tongue grass, are responsible for the common name. Although it can be weedy in small gardens, the tawny mass of foliage persists attractively through winter in dry or moist meadows.

Bottlebrush grass, **Hystrix patula**, appropriately named for the structure of its terminal flower clusters, and wild-oats, **Chasmanthium latifolium**, which produces flat oatlike pendulous flower spikes, are native to woodlands in the eastern states. Both are well suited to shady gardens, although wild-oats does equally well in full sun with adequate moisture, its autumn leaves turning to gold and its flower spikes to salmon-brown.

American grasses, like much of our American flora, have been underexplored as to their garden potential, often being passed over in favor of exotic species. With renewed interest in our own floral heritage, many native garden gems are coming to light; for instance, a number of species of plume grass (*Erianthus* spp.) which inhabit moist soil on the Coastal Plain from New York south to Florida and west to Kentucky. Narrowly upright, and varying in height from six feet (bent-awn plume grass, **Erianthus contortus**) to over nine feet (sugarcane plume grass, **E. giganteus**), these elegant, stately grasses are topped by plumelike flower clusters which are effective all winter. Fall foliage is red to dark purple. All are well adapted to sunny positions in average garden soils.

Our West Coast flora also includes a number of clump-forming grasses, little-known but superbly suited to garden use. Highlights are: California fescue, **Festuca californica**, with bluish leaves to two feet tall on dry open ground in Oregon and California; deergrass, **Muhlenbergia rigens**, a southern California native producing whiplike flower panicles in summer or fall; and pacific reed grass, **Calamagrostis nutkaensis**, a native from California to Alaska, whose reedlike flower clusters change gradually from purple-bronze to beige. ❧

71

GARDEN IN THE WOODS

DAVID R. LONGLAND

Wild phlox and yellow lady's-slipper pro
a striking contrast in this woodland settin

G arden in the Woods is a dream in the realization, a year's long dream about a big wild flower sanctuary in which plants will be grown, their likes and dislikes discovered, and the knowledge gained passed on in an effort to curb the wholesale destruction of our most beautiful natives. This is to be our contribution to conservation." Proclaiming this their mission in 1934, Garden cofounders Will Curtis and Howard "Dick" Stiles began to gather and grow botanical treasures from all over North America.

Will Curtis purchased the Garden property in 1931, greatly inspired by its diverse, glacier-carved terrain of winding eskers, streams and kettlehole ponds. Trained as a landscape designer at Cornell University, Curtis felt strongly about the romantic appeal of naturalistic gardens. Dick Stiles, inspired by Curtis' enthusiasm and determination, became an avid horticulturist with a special flair for garden design. Over the course of four decades, these men established thousands of wildflowers, ferns, shrubs and trees in both natural and modified settings on this remarkable property.

DAVID R. LONGLAND, *as director of Garden in the Woods in Framingham, MA, oversees the management and development of garden programs and operations. He has special interests in native plants, garden design and habitat restoration.*

In order to secure their "dream in the realization," Curtis and Stiles entrusted the Garden to the New England Wild Flower Society in 1965. The Society's chartered purpose was to promote the horticulture and conservation of native American plants through education and research. Today, as the Society's botanical garden and headquarters, Garden in the Woods contains the largest landscaped collection of wildflowers in the Northeast. The Garden has become one of the nation's chief conserva-

cultural symphony of contrasting forms, textures and seasonal colors at Garden in the Woods. Trails meander over 45 rolling acres, where 1500 varieties of wild plants flourish in a series of specially designed, naturalistic gardens: Rich Woodland Groves, Lily Pond, Rockeries, Sunny Bog, Pine Barrens, Meadow, Western Scree and Laurel Bend—a unique display of drought-tolerant wildflowers for dry New England landscapes.

The Garden's horticultural staff grows both rare and common wildflowers for display, for sale to visitors, and for conservation and research. In keeping with the original purpose of Garden in the Woods, "the knowledge so gained" is disseminated through lectures and publications which promote the conservation of native American flora. The New England Wildflower Society sponsors a great variety of educational programs at the Garden, in response to the wide range of interests expressed by members and visitors.

From spring through fall, Garden in the Woods offers a kaleidoscopic succession of colorful wildflowers, including: liverworts (*Hepatica* spp.) and trailing arbutus (*Epigaea repens*) in April; lady's-slippers (*Cypripedium* spp.) and trilliums (*Trillium* spp.) in May; prickly pears (*Opuntia* spp.) and pitcher plants (*Sarracenia* spp.) in June; Turk's cap lilies, (*Lilium superbum*) and blazing stars (*Liatrus* spp.) in July; Cardinal flowers (*Lobelia cardinalis*) and turtleheads (*Chelone* spp.) in August; and aster (*Asters* spp.) gentians (*Gentiana* spp.) and brilliant foliage in autumn.

Garden trails are open daily from 9 a.m. to 4 p.m. *except Mondays*, April 15 to October 31, and an admission fee is charged to non-members. The offices and library are open Tuesday through Friday, 9 a.m. to 4 p.m. year-round. 🍂

FOR MORE INFORMATION CONTACT:
Garden in the Woods
Hemenway Road Framingham, MA 01701
(617) 877-7630; 237-4924

tors of rare native plants, such as Oconee bells, (*Shortia galacifolia*), spreading globe-flower, and climbing fern (*Lygodium palmatum*). Also, the Garden is a showcase of unusual cultivars of wild plants like albino cardinal flower, (*Lobelia cardinalis* 'Alba'), double-flowered trillium (*Trillium grandiflorum* forma *petalosum*) and blood-root, dwarf hemlocks, (*Tsuga canadensis* cultivars), variegated wild oats (*Uvularia sessilifolia* 'Variegata') and many others.

Visitors who appreciate the regenerative spirit of nature and art will revel in a horti-

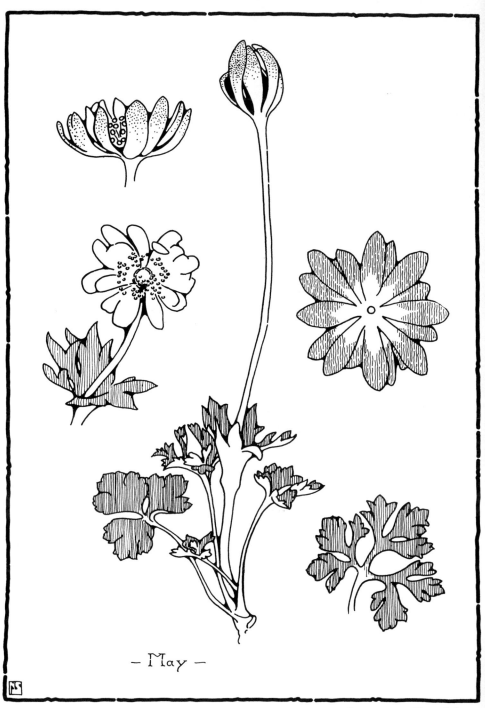

— May —

NORTH CAROLINA BOTANICAL GARDEN

KEN MOORE

A visit to the North Carolina Botanical Garden will provide opportunities to enjoy and learn about native plants in a variety of natural and cultivated settings.

The Garden administers 598 acres of forests and open lands, much of which is managed to preserve the diversity of the regional flora and fauna for public appreciation and University teaching and research. Approximately 100 acres are traversed by nature trails through the local Piedmont forest. Ten acres are under intensive cultivation, including the Garden's historic and beautiful four-acre Coker Arboretum in the center of the campus of The University of North Carolina at Chapel Hill. At the time of this writing, the Garden, under the leadership of Garden Director, Dr. Peter S. White, is involved in master planning and landscape design work. This means by the time you visit, you may be watching the construction of a new visitors' center or the expansion of the native plant Habitat Gardens. At whatever time you may visit the Garden, you will see native plants in quantity, and staff or volunteers are available to provide answers to specific inquiries.

The Habitat Gardens are the heart of the native plant collections. Plants characteristic of the North Carolina

mountains, coastal plain and sandhills are displayed in an acre of simulated habitat plantings. Walking through these distinct areas a visitor may experience a sense of being in the larger natural area represented. The Mountain Habitat Garden is a shady area of hemlocks and tulip-poplars with mountain laurels and rhododendrons providing a setting for many ferns and wildflowers characteristic of the western counties of North Carolina. Trilliums and other mountain wildflowers are at peak bloom during April and May each year.

The Coastal Plain and the Sandhills Habitat Gardens, both of which are open to the sun, make the Mountain Habitat Garden, in contrast, an inviting cool retreat during hot summer days. Fire is used as a seasonal part of the management of the Coastal Plain and Sandhills Habitats because, in nature, such habitats are subjected to fires on a much larger scale. Fire used as a management tool at the Garden demonstrates to the public that fires, in certain situations, are beneficial. In the case of the Coastal Plain Habitat, fire maintains the open habitat necessary for the survival of many wildflowers such as fringed orchids and pitcher plants. Visitors during September and October, even after early frosts, are surprised to find the Coastal Plain Habitat Garden at its peak with masses of blue, yellow and white flowers of species characteristic of the eastern lowland counties of the state. The Sandhills Habitat is characterized

KEN MOORE *is assistant director of the North Carolina Botanical Garden. He has been a leader in work with native wildflowers and a major force behind the Garden's "Conservation through Propagation" and "Wildflower of the Year" programs.*

throughout the year by the exposed white sandridges towered over by long-leaf pines (*Pinus palustris*) and scrubby turkey oaks (*Quercus laevis*) so characteristic of this particular part of North Carolina.

Wildflower borders situated around the Totten Center visitor area are of peak interest beginning with wild columbine (*Aquilegia canadensis*) in April and ending with masses of goldenrod (*Solidago* spp.) and blue and white asters (*Aster* spp.) in mid-October. These wildflower borders demonstrate that there are many wildflowers and "roadside weeds" appropriate for home gardens and urban landscapes. The "Wildflower of the Year," a wildflower species selected cooperatively each year by the North Carolina Botanical Garden and The Garden Club of North Carolina, Inc., is prominently displayed in the wildflower borders. The "Wildflower of the Year" project is a conservation activity, one of many of the Garden's "Conservation Through Propagation" programs, which promotes an easy to propagate and cultivate North Carolina wildflower each year. For example, cardinal flower, *Lobelia cardinalis*, which was the first species selected, is displayed in several locations to attract hummingbirds from July through September. During the growing season, plants and seeds of the "Wildflower of the Year" are available to visitors.

The carnivorous plants are the most popular and entertaining. *Dionaea muscipula*, Venus's-flytrap, is the most famous plant at the Garden. It occurs throughout the Coastal Plain Habitat Garden, as it occurs in nature in the coastal plain of North and South Carolina and nowhere else in the world. It flowers in early June. There are numerous flytraps in the carnivorous plant display bed, where visitors, young and old alike, enjoy "fooling" the plants into action. Visitors learn how to trick the plant by reading the

Fall colors at the sandhills habitat section of the North Carolina Botanical Garden. PHOTO BY JAMES WARD

labels placed around the display beds. The carnivorous plants collection at the Garden includes pitcher plants (*Sarracenia* spp.), sundews (*Drosera* spp.) and butterworts (*Pinguicula* spp.) native to the southeastern U.S. Visitors will learn that some are very rare and that the habitat of these interesting plants are generally threatened by various activities of society throughout our nation. The Garden's propagation program provides the visitor with opportunities to observe seedling carnivorous plants as well as hybrids.

Visitors interested in gardening with native plants will find a wealth of information by making inquiries of the Garden staff. Printed materials relative to wildflower propagation and cultivation, sources of plants and seed, and other pertinent information are available upon inquiry. A limited selection of propagated wildflowers are generally available for purchase through the courtesy of the Garden volunteers who are very active in supporting the propagation and conservation activities of the Garden.

Native plants are also displayed throughout the Plant Families Garden, where visitors observe that plants such as the native atamasco lily (*Zephyranthes atamasco*), garlic chives and asparagus are very closely related to the lily family. Another of many interesting families displayed is the aster, or composite family, which includes the goldenrods, ragweeds, blackeyed Susans and horticulturally bred marigolds and zinnias.

Native plants displayed throughout the Mercer Reeves Hubbard Herb Garden vary from poison ivy, oak and sumac (*Rhus* spp.) in the poison garden to Jack-in-the-pulpit (*Arisaema triphyllum*) which occurs in the poison, medicinal and American native herbs section of this comprehensive garden of plants of value for society.

Hours of visitation for the special collections around the Totten Center are Monday-Friday excluding holidays.

Cardinal flower (*Lobelia cardinalis*) never fails to attract hummingbirds to the North Carolina Botanical Garden.

Weekend hours from mid-March-mid-November are 10 a.m.-5 p.m. Saturdays and 2-5 p.m. Sundays.

The Garden maintains an active schedule of educational programs, field trips and special events throughout the year. These are described in advance in the Garden's bimonthly newsletter which is distributed to members of the Botanical Garden Foundation.

Information on these activities and on scheduling group tours and appointments with staff may be obtained by writing the Education Coordinator, North Carolina Botanical Garden, 3375 Totten Center, University of North Carolina at Chapel Hill, Chapel Hill, North Carolina 27599-3375 or by calling 919-967-2246 weekdays, 8 a.m. to 5 p.m. ❧

THE CROSBY ARBORETUM

PICAYUNE, MISSISSIPPI

CHRIS J. WELLS

With greater value being placed on our natural heritage, The Crosby Arboretum is a treasure of the Gulf South region. It allows us to learn about native plants and plant products so that we may use them to their best advantage while ensuring their genetic perpetuation. Through The Crosby Arboretum, aesthetic, agricultural, scientific and industrial contributions of native plants and ecosystems can be examined in a real-life setting.

Since its beginning in 1979, The Crosby Arboretum has become a premier native plant repository for the region. The Arboretum protects the region's biological diversity and provides a place for the public to enjoy plants native to the Pearl River Drainage Basin. The Crosby Arboretum uniquely provides for the study and enjoyment of plants in their original habitat.

The Arboretum consists of the 64-acre

Pinecote, the Native Plant Center of The Crosby Arboretum, adjacent to Interstate 59 south of Picayune, Mississippi. The displays within the Center are naturalistic plant communities reflecting the beauty and diversity of the region. Each is designed to display the successional changes through which a natural plant system may pass. Fire is used at Pinecote and natural areas as an essential management technique for pine savannas and bogs.

Pinecote includes the Piney Woods Lake where native water plants furnish habitat for aquatic wildlife and waterfowl. Built to complement both artistic and functional aspects, Pinecote Pavilion was designed by internationally known architect Fay Jones, of Fayetteville, Arkansas. The pavilion, bridges and other architectural amenities are designed in harmony with nature. Thus, Pinecote is used for the quiet, reflective enjoyment of nature, as well as a gathering place for activities.

Other Arboretum sites, known as natural areas, allow the visitor to gain an appreciation of completely natural habitats. From sandy hills and open longleaf pine woodlands to slash pine savannas and exotic pitcher plant bogs, the fire-maintained communities provide a vigorous and ever-

CHRIS J. WELLS *is the superintendent and botanist for The Crosby Arboretum. He began his formal botanical education upon leaving the U.S. Navy in 1974 and entering Northwestern State University in Natchitoches, LA. As an undergraduate he accompanied several botanical expeditions to Latin America. In 1984, he accepted his position with the Crosby Arboretum and received his masters degree in biological sciences from Mississippi State University.*

SAND-HILL SUNFLOWER

changing display of wildflowers. In contrast, the old-growth of cypress swamps, bottom lands and beech-magnolia forests protects flowers and wildlife rarely seen. Carnivorous plants and orchids are commonly found in many of the Arboretum's natural habitats. This vast assemblage of carefully selected and protected natural areas nurtures over 700 species of trees, shrubs, wildflowers and grasses found in the Pearl River Basin of southern Mississippi and southeast Louisiana.

The Arboretum maintains an expanding library, and a quarterly news journal informs members of timely happenings and helps readers gain knowledge of the natural environment. *Arboreports* are short, serial reports on sharply focused topics which include garden concept, resource management, environmental issues and scientific research. Special publications include the Native Plant Series consisting of the *Checklist of the Woody Plant Species of the Pearl River Drainage Basin* and the *Guide to the Natural Areas of The Crosby Arboretum.*

The Arboretum Gift Shop offers objects created by regional artisans including pine needle baskets and other articles relating to botanical themes.

Educational programs focus upon the arts, sciences and the humanities. The Arboretum also provides mini-grants to aid teachers in developing programs that will enhance their students' opportunities to learn about and experience the natural world.

The Crosby Arboretum is founded on the philosophy that plants are more than attractive features of our landscape; plants are an integral part of the environment; our own survival will be threatened if they do not flourish. Therefore, mankind's best interests can be served by the study of our plant neighbors with which we share this planet.

FOR MORE INFORMATION CONTACT:

The Crosby Arboretum
1801 Goodyear Boulevard
Picayune, MS 39466
(601) 798-6961

THE ARBORETUM AT FLAGSTAFF

ARIZONA

WAYNE A. HITE

The Arboretum, with its wondrous view of the imposing San Francisco Peaks, was established in 1981 as a center for native plant research and exhibition. Located just outside Flagstaff, Arizona, the Arboretum occupies 200 acres of ponderosa pine forest land at an elevation of 7,150 feet and includes a fascinating diversity of plants native to alpine tundra, coniferous forest and high desert. The Arboretum is also involved in a nationwide program for conservation of threatened and endangered plants.

The northern Arizona climate is a chal-

WAYNE HITE *has bachelor and masters degrees in forest ecology. He worked in forest land management, planning and research prior to becoming the executive director of The Arboretum at Flagstaff in 1985.*

lenge for local growers. The area is characterized by spring droughts, summer rains and cold, snowy winters. The site can experience a frost during 11 months of the year. The humidity is quite low each day. These climatic conditions have made it difficult to grow many of the widely cultivated species of plants.

At the Arboretum, we are promoting many native shrubs and herbaceous plants now offered at regional nurseries. Of particular note are the many species of penstemon (*Penstemon* spp.) and columbine (*Aquilegia* spp.). Found throughout the 170,000-square-mile. Colorado Plateau, these hardy species offer a wide variety of flower colors and plant sizes.

We've also introduced gardeners to the

The Arboretum occupies 200 acres of ponderosa pine forest land at an elevation of 7,150 feet.

local ground cover, pussytoes (*Antennaria* spp.). Low-growing, gray-green-leaved perennials, these species are well adapted to the intense sunlight, extreme temperature ranges and low annual precipitation of northern Arizona.

Endangered plants are mixed into the plantings on the grounds. They include shrubs such as Arizona cliff-rose (*Cowania subintegra*) and Arizona willow (*Salix arizonica*) and herbs exemplified by Goodings onion (*Allium goodingii*) and San Francisco peaks groudsel (*Senecio franciscanus*).

The Arboretum is located at the crossroads of many interesting vegetation types that typify the high elevation and dry environments of the American West.

The Arboretum reaches schoolchildren, gardeners and scientists through educational programs. Large-scale community events are scheduled during the summer to teach people about the value of resource conservation and the richness of the Colorado Plateau flora.

The Arboretum is open Monday through Friday, 10 a.m. to 3 p.m. year-round and on Saturdays in June, July and August. ❦

FOR MORE INFORMATION CONTACT:
The Arboretum at Flagstaff
P.O. Box 670
Flagstaff, AZ 86002
(602) 774-1441

81

RESTORED PRAIRIES

OF THE UNIVERSITY OF WISCONSIN

MADISON ARBORETUM

VIRGINIA M. KLINE

Prairie wildflowers abound in the restored prairies of the University of Wisconsin Madison Arboretum and are easily observed from the fire-lanes and walking trails. Here plants with unfamiliar names such as rattlesnake master (*Eryngium yuccifolium*), prairie dock (*Silphium terebinthinaceum*) and prairie gayfeather (*Liatris pycnostachya*) grow among big and little bluestem (*Andropogon gerardii* and *Schizachyrium scoparium*), prairie dropseed (*Sporobolis heterolepis*), Indian grass (*Sorghastrum nutans*) and other prairie grasses much as they did when the first settlers arrived here 150 years ago.

There are over 300 plant species in Cur-

VIRGINIA KLINE *is staff ecologist and research program manager at the University of Wisconsin Arboretum. She is a community ecologist who received her Ph.D. in botany from the University of Wisconsin-Madison in 1976. Much of her research relates to the restoration and management of natural communities. For the past 11 years she has coordinated research at the Arboretum and has been responsible for planning and evaluating the management of the Arboretum's collection of biotic communities.*

tis Prairie and Henry Greene Prairie, the largest of the Arboretum's restored prairies. Curtis Prairie (60 acres) is the oldest restored tall-grass prairie in the world. Once cropland, it was a horse pasture when acquired by the Arboretum in 1933. Planting of prairie sods, seedling transplants and seeds was accomplished with the help of Civilian Conservation Corps (CCC) labor in the late 1930's. This is the site where some of the earliest prescribed burning experiments were carried out, which demonstrated the beneficial effects of fire and laid the groundwork for the widely adopted prescribed burn practices of today.

Henry Greene Prairie (40 acres) was named for the botanist who almost single-handedly planted the prairie, most of it between 1945 and 1952. While Curtis Prairie is on silt loam soils, the soils in Greene Prairie are sandy, varying from very dry to wet, or poorly drained clay. This provides habitat for many species that do not grow in Curtis Prairie.

The objective of the Arboretum prairie

- July -

restoration is to re-create a small sample of the once widespread but now rare prairie community, for use in teaching and research. It is a complex community of plants and animals, and attempting to put the parts together has led to greater understanding of the interactions of the plants and animals and their environment.

Prairies are dominated by grasses, and more than a dozen species of grass can be found in the Arboretum prairies. Tallest and most characteristic of the tallgrass prairies is big bluestem or turkeyfoot grass. On the deep silt loams of Curtis Prairie it grows eight feet or more in a good year after a spring burn. Other tall species include Indian grass and switch grass (*Panicum virgatum*), and, on wetter soils, bluejoint grass (*Calamagrostis canadensis*) and cordgrass (*Spartina pectinata*). However, perhaps more suitable for most home prairie gardens are the shorter species. These include little bluestem, prairie dropseed, sideoats grama grass (*Bouteloua curtipendula*) and the small panic grasses

(for example, *Dichanthelium leibergii* and *D. oligosanthes*).

Interspersed among the grasses are species of many other families, composites and legumes being particularly well represented. All are adapted to drought, wind and high light intensity. The plants grow close together, with as many as ten different species in a square yard. Flowering is staggered among the species, so that the prairie changes in aspect as the season progresses and something is always in flower. In general shorter plants flower early and tall plants later. The seedheads of those that have matured and the foliage of those yet to flower add interest and diversity.

Prairies require no fertilization or irrigation, but burning is essential. Each Arboretum prairie is generally burned (twice) in a three or four year period, usually in early spring when the plants are dormant. Early spring burns stimulate growth and flowering of the grasses and many of the wildflowers, so the prairies are most showy the year of a spring burn.

The Grady Tract at the University of Wisconsin Madison with butterfly weed, pearly everlasting and false indigo in bloom.

Among the earliest flowers in spring are pasqueflower (*Pulsatilla patens,* formerly *Anemone patens*) and bird's foot violet (*Viola pedata*), which grow in dry sandy soil. Soon to follow are prairie smoke (*Geum triflorum*), with its unusual closed red flowers and rosettes of hairy, dissected leaves, the blue spikes of lupine (*Lupinus perennis*) and the pink and white shooting stars (*Dodecatheon meadia*) with their gracefully reflexed petals, the flowers held high above the basal rosette of ephemeral leaves.

Early summer brings tall white wild indigo (*Baptisia lactea,* formerly *B. leucantha*) and other legumes: leadplant (*Amorpha canescens*) with attractive gray foliage and small purple flowers, and the prairie clovers (*Dalea purpurea* and *D. candida*—both of these were formerly in the genus *Petalostemum*) with short spikes of magenta or white flowers held above finely divided leaves. Butterflyweed (*Asclepias tuberosa*) adds a splash of intense orange. In

July the open clusters of small, pure white flowers of flowering spurge (*Euphorbia corollata*) appear; their delicate texture will enhance the prairie for many weeks. Rattlesnake master, a strange plant with leaves like a yucca and tight spherical heads of greenish white flowers also begins to flower in July.

The big show of composites begins with pale purple coneflower (*Echinacea pallida*) and early sunflower (*Heliopsis helianthoides*), to be followed later in summer by yellow coneflower (*Ratibida pinnata*), vivid magenta spikes of gayfeather, and the tall stalks of yellow sunflowerlike heads of compass plant (*Silphium laciniatum*), and prairie dock. The huge basal leaves of both compass plant and prairie dock tend to be oriented so that the narrow edges face the noon sun, thus avoiding direct sunlight at the hottest time of day. Their size, shape and orientation make the leaves conspicuous in the prairie throughout the summer.

The Henry Greene Prairie at the arboretum is filled with many different grasses. Here the large leaves of prairie dock, *Silphium terebinthinaceum*, stand above the grasses.

Ten species of asters, such as smooth aster (*Aster laevis*) and New England aster (*A. novae-angliae*), and seven species of goldenrod, including stiff goldenrod (*Solidago rigida*) with its flat-topped inflorescence, and showy goldenrod (*S. speciosa*) with its spikelike one, are conspicuous composites in late summer and fall.

While individual species are interesting, and many (including those mentioned here) can be grown in the garden, it is the combinations of grasses and forbs, varying in space and time, that give the prairie its distinctive appeal. Walking the trails through the Arboretum prairies, visitors are given a chance to observe and enjoy many of these combinations, which may provide inspiration for natural landscape plantings and prairie gardens.

The University of Wisconsin-Madison Arboretum is unique in its emphasis on restoration of native communities.

Although there is a 60-acre horticultural area, the Longenecker Garden, with an outstanding display of lilacs and flowering crabapples, most of the 1,280-acre site is used for the development of examples of the different types of forests, savannas, prairies and wetlands that were present in presettlement Wisconsin. These areas are used for teaching and research, with special emphasis on the restoration process. Free public tours are given on weekends. During the summer, the prairies are highlighted. Group tours can be arranged. Maps and information are available at the McKay Center in the Arboretum. 🌱

FOR MORE INFORMATION CONTACT:

**The University of Wisconsin
Madison Aboretum
1207 Seminole Highway
Madison, WI 53711
(608) 262-2746**

THE CONNECTICUT COLLEGE ARBORETUM
N E W   L O N D O N

SALLY TAYLOR

The Connecticut College Arboretum was established on 64 acres by George Avery in 1931 in southeastern Connecticut outside the small city of New London. The original plan of the Arboretum "dramatized an existing grove of ancient hemlocks which grew atop a 40-foot granite cliff." The hemlock grove was given to the College in 1911 by a New London family who had owned it since the 1600s; the land was originally bought from Owaneco, the son of the Mohican Indian Chief Uncas. The ravine, cliff and hemlock setting dominated the old farm site (which was crossed by colonial stone walls) with its dramatic, magnificent granite outcroppings and glacial boulder train. The topography was well suited to become an arboretum, with gently rolling hills and small valleys. One rock-strewn depression, a red maple swamp, became a pond when the small stream was dammed and seasonal flooding created a focal point and backdrop for subsequent construction of the formal entrance opening onto the stately Laurel Walk.

The only building in the Arboretum is Buck Lodge, constructed of fieldstone and cedar, which is nearby the Outdoor Theatre. The Lodge, which has simple facilities and a magnificent stone fireplace is available to the public by arrangement

through the Botany Department Office. The Outdoor Theatre was created with stage, "wings" and seating area to serve as a location for dance production and College exercises. In 1938, a hurricane struck New London directly, and all but six of the 130 magnificent hemlocks up to three feet in diameter were blown down. Only those growing within the ravine were spared. As time passed, regeneration of the oak/beech/maple forest surrounding the hemlocks repaired the scars, and little evidence of the disaster remains except for the massive throw mounds and decayed trunks of the fallen giants. Paths lead to the area from the Williams Street entrance. Today the Arboretum has grown to approximately 425 acres, including habitats as diverse as a true bog and a salt marsh connecting a rocky wooded island in the Thames River to the mainland.

The plant collection's emphasis remains the study and preservation of woody species native to New England. The 20 acres closest to the Main Entrance and the Laurel Walk contain flowering shrubs and trees of the rose, legume, heath and honeysuckle families as well as a woodland wildflower garden which is connected to a newly created Conifer Garden.

The azalea collection includes all of the native species which will grow in our area. The original plantings of pinxter flower (*Rhododendron periclymenoides*), rose-shell azalea (*R. prinophyllum*), swamp azalea (*R. viscosum*) and flame azalea (*R. calendulaceum*) flank paths leading past the Laurel

SALLY TAYLOR *has been in the Department of Botany at Connecticut College for 25 years and associated with the Arboretum for 20 years. Her special interests are native azaleas and the use of native shrubs and trees in ornamental garden plantings. She has also served as a guest editor for* **P&G**.

Walk with its backdrop of massive rosebay rhododendron (*R. maximum*). These 50-year-old plants flower during May and late June in the high shade of large tulip trees and red maples. A newer collection includes rhodora (*R. canadense*), plum leaf azalea (*R. prunifolium*) and coast azalea (*R. atlanticum*) as well as evergreen Carolina rhododendron (*R. carolinianum*). The plum leaf azalea creates a startling display of orange-red flowers in late July and August.

Early to mid-June is the best time to visit the new collection of mountain laurel cultivars (*Kalmia latifolia*), which flower at the same time as the plants along the original Laurel Walk. The wild laurels with pale pink to deep pink buds and flowers have been hybridized by Richard Jaynes and others to produce plants with scarlet buds and flowers intricately banded in red. Leaves vary in shape and color from normal, dull-green oval to narrow, willowlike and glossy.

One demonstration naturalistic landscaping area contains native silverbell (*Halesia tetraptera*, formerly *H. carolina*), flowering in May, yellowwood (*Cladrastis kentukea*) flowering in June, and sourwood (*Oxydendrum arboreum*), flowering in August. A second larger area features high-bush blueberry (*Vaccinium corymbosum*), and a 50-year-old huckleberry (*Gaylussacia baccata*) clone which has been maintained by techniques of naturalistic landscaping pioneered by the Arboretum.

The favorite shrub of the Arboretum collection is the native highbush blueberry. We call it the aristocrat of our native shrubs because of its broad seasonal interest which includes red winter twigs, small bell-like flowers in spring, glossy foliage in summer, blue fruits and colorful foliage in fall. The blueberry branching structures is naturally contorted because the twigs have false terminal buds, each year growing at a slight angle from the stem, creating a zig-zag appearance to the branches when they are young. Mature plants may be pruned to emphasize this character. We feature sev-eral of these older plants in the Naturalistic Landscape areas, and blueberries have been used successfully as ornamental plants near campus buildings. Highbush blueberry is not a clonal plant and it tends to remain single-stemmed, unlike its cousins of the blueberry barrens of northern New England.

The notable small tree to see in the Arboretum in fall and late summer is sourwood (*Oxydendrum arboreum*). Long after most flowering trees have made their showing, its long slender clusters of white bells appear, giving a clue to its relationship with the native andromeda. The appearance of the flowers in late July is a welcome addition to the sequence of flowering trees. The flowers are followed by small capsules which persist until the leaves have dropped, giving the tree the unusual appearance of continuous flowering. The leaves are long oval, glossy green, and somewhat leathery. They begin to turn to the characteristic deep red by the first of September, and remain on the tree making a brilliant show until the last fall color has gone from the landscape.

Sourwood ranges in size from a large shrub to a medium-sized tree and is unusual in flowering profusely when it is young and small. Its form tends to be narrow and vertical when young, with leaves clothing the branches low to the ground, so it rapidly makes a satisfactory specimen tree. Coloring is most brilliant in full sun, less so in semi-shade. ❦

Literature Cited

The Connecticut Arboretum: Its First Fifty Years, 1931-1981 Bulletin 28, Connecticut College, New London. 1982. 56 pp.

FOR MORE INFORMATION CONTACT:

Glenn Dreyer, Director
Connecticut College Arboretum
Connecticut College
New London, CT 06320
(203) 447-1911, x7700.

WILDFLOWER AND NATIVE PLANT GARDEN

BRANDYWINE CONSERVANCY

BRANDYWINE RIVER MUSEUM,

CHADDS FORD, PA

F. M. MOOBERRY

Surrounding the Brandywine River Museum is an extensive wildflower and native plant garden which exemplifies the Brandywine Conservancy's purpose to preserve, utilize and display artistic, natural and historical resources of the Brandywine region.

The display garden is filled with wildflowers that are easy to grow and suitable for property owners to raise in their gardens. Plants are chosen to match the habitat rather than changing habitat to suit the plants. A large number of sun-loving species grace the parking lot's islands and are an important and integral part of the native plantings. A succession of blooming plants begins early in April with bloodroot, *Sanguinaria canadensis*, and ends in late November with the last wildflower of the year, fringed gentian, *Gentianopsis crinita*.

The artists represented in the fine arts collection of the Brandywine River

F.M. MOOBERRY *has been coordinator of horticulture for the Brandywine Conservancy and River Museum, Chadds Ford, PA since 1977. Her responsibilities involve both cultivated and natural areas; she manages design, maintenance and propagation for wildflower and native plant gardens. She conducts environmental impact surveys and provides meadow-management expertise for Conservancy and other lands. She is author of Brandywine Wildflowers and co-author of Grow Native Shrubs in Your Garden.*

Museum often used wildflowers as subjects. Many of these wildflowers are included in the garden.

Blooming shrubs and native flowering trees add to nature's pulsebeat as spring unfolds. Bluebells, *Mertensia virginica*, grow in beautiful profusion on the floodplain of the Brandywine and are featured plants of the spring wildflower garden. Their trumpetlike flowers are pink in bud and then turn sky blue as they open. A native plant that adapts well to the home garden, this perennial becomes dormant, dying back to the ground and vanishing completely from sight by midsummer, not emerging until its purple leaves and buds break through soil the following April.

Foamflower (*Tiarella cordifolia*), wild bleeding heart (*Dicentra eximia*), green and gold (*Chrysogonum virginianum*), wild ginger (*Asarum canadense*), wood poppy (*Stylophorum diphyllum*), Jacob's-ladder (*Polemonium reptans*), Miami mist (*Phacelia purshii*) and native azaleas (*Rhododendron* spp.) are additional spring favorites.

All regional habitats are represented in the garden, from full sun to deep shade, rich to thin sterile soils, from dry to standing water sites. An essential part of the garden is the Museum parking lot's water run-off retention basin which varies in

At the Brandywine Museum a succession of blooming plants begins early in April and ends in late November with the last wildflower of the year. Blooming shrubs and native flowering trees add to nature's pulsebeat.

depth and provides a habitat for spring's wild blue iris (*Iris versicolor*), golden ragwort (*Senecio aureus*), and summer's swamp rose-mallow (*Hibiscus palustris*), followed by fall's cardinal flower (*Lobelia cardinalis*) and blue lobelia (*L. siphilitica*), all species that love moisture.

Summer brings the brilliant butterfly weed (*Asclepias tuberosa*) as well as the Turk's-cap and Canada lily (*Lilium superbum*) and (*L. canadense*), wild bergamot (*Monarda fistulosa*) and blazing star (*Liatris spicata*).

Four plants sharing the same common name, black-eyed Susan, are all in the genus *Rudbeckia* (*R. hirta, speciosa, triloba* and *fulgida*). These plants provide an extended sequence of blooms of different forms, textures and sizes.

The month of September is host to New York ironweed (*Vernonia noveboracensis*) and Joe-Pye weed (*Eupatorium fistulosum*). Continuing in bloom from late summer are the long-flowering trumpet vine (*Campsis radicans*) and turtle head (*Chelone glabra*).

New England aster (*Aster novae-angliae*) and the frost asters (*Aster* spp.) combine with goldenrods (*Solidago* spp.), which bloom in both sun and shade, for a glorious finale in October and November.

Over 250 species of wildflowers, shrubs and trees are to be found in the gardens, all easily propagated and adaptable for use by home gardeners.

The Conservancy's volunteers promote the conservation of wildflowers and native plants. To accomplish this important goal, the garden volunteers collect, clean and package over 100 different wildflower seeds. These are used for growing plants for the garden and are also packaged for sale to the public in the Museum shop.

Another important objective is the propagation program of native plants which culminates in a popular May plant sale. This sale enables the home gardener to purchase plants that were grown from seed rather than collected from wild populations. The volunteers also maintain a garden cart full of blooming plants which are available for purchase during the remainder of the gardening season.

Guided garden tours are available. 🦋

FOR MORE INFORMATION CONTACT:
The Brandywine River Museum
Brandywine Conservancy
Route 1 and Route 100
Chadds Ford, PS 19317
(215) 459-1900

NATIONAL WILDFLOWER RESEARCH CENTER

BETH ANDERSON

Lady Bird Johnson and a corps of concerned citizens created the National Wildflower Research Center in response to a growing awareness that our native vegetation was rapidly disappearing. The inaugural gift establishing the Center came from Mrs. Johnson in the form of $125,000 and sixty acres of land on the Colorado River near Austin, Texas.

The Wildflower Center is dedicated to promoting the preservation and increased use of wildflowers and native plants. The Center's primary focus is on research and education. Of the some 20,000 species of flowering plants in North America, only a fraction have been studied in depth. Landscaping success with wildflowers and native plants is not always predictable, as so little is known about their cultivation. More research is needed. Through experiments at the Center and in cooperative projects across the country, a database of information is being established. By studying the growth habits and requirements of our native species we can learn more about how to use them in commercial and residential landscapes.

The Wildflower Center's Clearinghouse serves as a network to join individuals and organizations working with native plants, by gathering up-to-date information on current research and wildflower projects in each state. This information is compiled into fact sheets on seed sources, recommended species, appropriate planting procedures for different regions of the country and additional resources for wildflower information. The Clearinghouse contains an impressive technical library and an extensive slide collection.

The Wildflower Center is working to preserve America's rich heritage of wildflowers and native plants. Increasing the use of hardy, drought-resistant, indigenous native plant species will allow us to have the best of all worlds. We can enjoy our landscaped areas; we can protect our water supply; we can increase ecological stability; and we can preserve the genetic information essential to the continued existence of native plants and our future utilization of them. Using native plants indigenous to a particular area also helps "each state to speak in its own regional accents," as Mrs. Johnson says.

In our efforts to educate the public about the need to protect and conserve this diminishing natural resource, we have developed a strong national membership program. A broad spectrum of professionals, and wildflower and native plant enthusiasts learn more about our native flora through membership in the Wildflower Center. Members receive a bimonthly newsletter; a biannual wildflower journal, written for the layman; reduced rates on educational seminars; and discounts on Center products.

Visitors to the Center can see over 300 labeled species native to the immediate region in designed landscape settings, in naturalistic community groupings — including a small established native prairie — and in more formal display plantings. Our research test plots and a new "Pollinator Garden" are also open. The Wildflower Center has color from late February through November and fact sheets and slide shows are offered year round. 🌸

FOR MORE INFORMATION CONTACT:
National Wildflower Research Center
2600 FM 973 North
Austin, TX 78725 (512) 929-3600

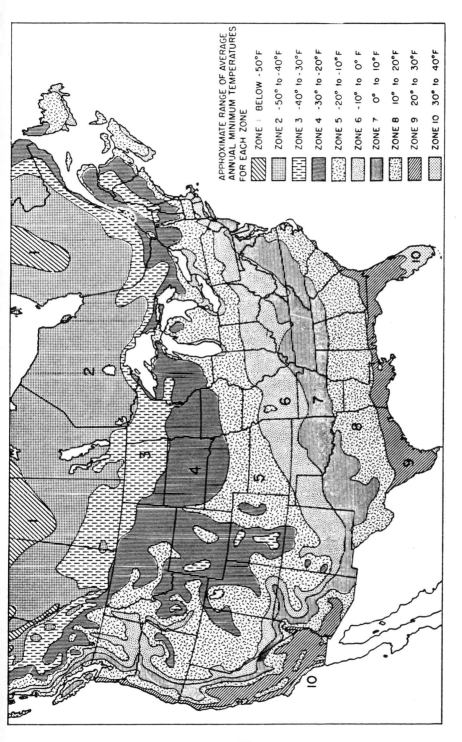

APPROXIMATE RANGE OF AVERAGE
ANNUAL MINIMUM TEMPERATURES
FOR EACH ZONE

ZONE 1   BELOW - 50°F
ZONE 2   - 50° to - 40°F
ZONE 3   - 40° to - 30°F
ZONE 4   - 30° to - 20°F
ZONE 5   - 20° to - 10°F
ZONE 6   - 10° to   0°F
ZONE 7   0° to 10°F
ZONE 8   10° to 20°F
ZONE 9   20° to 30°F
ZONE 10   30° to 40°F

Helpful Lists of Sources of Native Plants

NURSERY SOURCES: NATIVE PLANTS AND WILDFLOWERS, 1987, 72 pages.

Compiled by the New England Wild Flower Society, Inc., Garden in the Woods, Hemenway Road, Framingham, MA 01701. Sections include a list of popular native plants and nursery sources; a list of 58 nurseries propagating native plants for Zones 4-6; and a list of other nurseries selling propagated native plants. Available for $4.95. This booklet has been updated on an annual basis.

SOURCES OF NATIVE SEEDS AND PLANTS, 1982

Available from the Soil Conservation Society of America, 7515 Northeast Ankeny Road, Ankeny, IA 50021-9764. Single copies $3.50 postpaid. Contains 272 different sources listed by state with comments describing the type of material they offer.

A SOURCE BOOK OF INFORMATION ON HORTI-CULTURALLY USEFUL NATIVE OR NATURALIZED PLANTS OF THE SOUTHEASTERN UNITED STATES, 1985, 87 pages.

James H. Horton, Editor. Prepared and published by Western Carolina University. Sections include: a list of individuals who have expertise in using native plants for beautification; a list of institutions that can serve as resources; a list of sources for native and naturalized species; a habitat key; and a list of references.

SOURCES OF NATIVE PLANTS AND WILDFLOWERS

A three-page list of sources of seed and propagated plants published by the Virginia Native Plant Society. For a copy send a self-addressed stamped envelope to VNPS—Orders, P.O. Box 844, Annandale, VA 22003.

COMMERCIAL SEED SOURCES FOR SOUTHEASTERN NATIVE PLANTS

A one-page list of sources that offer propagated plants native to the southeastern U.S Published by the North Carolina Botanic Garden, UNC-CH, Totten Center 457A, Chapel Hill, NC 27514.

SOURCE LIST OF NATIVE PLANTS

A list of addresses of Western nurseries available from the Native Plant Society of New Mexico, P.O. Box 5917, Santa Fe, NM 87502. Send a self-addressed stamped envelope.

SOME SOURCES OF PLANT MATERIAL INDIGENOUS TO PINELANDS AREAS, 1981-1982.

Available for $1.50 from South Jersey Resource Conservation and Development Council, P.O. Box 676, Hammonton, NJ 08037.

SOME SOURCES OF PLANT MATERIAL NATIVE OR ADAPTED TO SEASHORE CONDITIONS, 1981-1982. Same as above.

TEXAS NATIVE PLANT DIRECTORIES

Contact the Texas Department of Agriculture, P.O. Box 12847, Austin, TX 78711.

ANDERSEN HORTICULTURAL LIBRARY'S SOURCE LIST OF PLANTS AND SEEDS, 1989, 214 pages.

A source list of over 40,000 entries of hardy plants (not exclusively native plants) listed by scientific name. Wholesale and mail-order nurseries are included. Available for $29.95 from: Andersen Horticultural Library, Minnesota Landscape Arboretum, 3675 Arboretum Drive, Box 39, Chanhassen, MN 55317.

NATIVE PLANT SOCIETIES

National Organizations

NATIONAL WILDFLOWER RESEARCH CENTER
2600 FM 973 North
Austin, TX 78725

OPERATION WILDFLOWER
NATIONAL COUNCIL OF STATE GARDEN CLUBS
Mrs. C. Norman Collard, Chairman
Box 860
Pocasset, MA 02559

SOIL CONSERVATION SOCIETY OF AMERICA
7515 Northeast Ankeny Road
Ankeny, IA 50021

THE CANADIAN WILDFLOWER SOCIETY
35 Bauer Crescent
Unionville, Ontario L3R 4H3

THE CENTER FOR PLANT CONSERVATION
The Arnold Arboretum
Harvard University
The Arborway
Jamaica Plain, MA 02130

THE NATURE CONSERVANCY
1800 North Kent Street, Suite 800
Arlington, VA 22209

State Groups

ALABAMA
Alabama Wildflower Society
c/o George Wood
Route 2, Box 115
Northport, AL 35476

ALASKA
Alaska Native Plant Society
P.O. Box 141613
Anchorage, AK 99514

ARIZONA
Arizona Native Plant Society
P.O. Box 41206 Sun Station
Tucson, AZ 85717

ARKANSAS
Arkansas Native Plant Society
c/o Mr. Don Peach
Route 1, Box 282
Mena, AR 71953

CALIFORNIA
California Botanical Society
c/o Department of Botany
University of California
Berkeley, CA 94720

California Native Plant Society
909 12th Street, Suite 116
Sacramento, CA 95814

California Native Plant Society Chapters:
Bristlecone (Inyo-Mono Region)
Channel Islands
Dorothy King Young (Coast from Jenner to
Ft. Bragg)
Kerr County
Marin
Milo Baker (Santa Rosa)
Monterey Bay
Mount Lassen
Napa Valley
North Coast
Northern San Joaquin Valley
Orange County
Riverside/San Bernadino Counties
Sacramento Valley
San Diego
San Francisco Bay
Sanhedrin (Ukiah)
San Luis Obispo County
Santa Clara Valley
Santa Cruz County
Santa Monica Mountains
Sequoia (Fresno)
Shasta
South Coast
Tahoe

National Alliance for Plants
c/o Alice Q. Howard
6415 Regent Street
Oakland, CA 94618
To improve rare plant protection.

Save-the-Redwoods League
114 Sansome Street, Room 605
San Francisco, CA 94104

COLORADO
Colorado Native Plant Society
Box 200
Fort Collins, CO 80522

CONNECTICUT
Connecticut Botanical Society
c/o Donald Swan
1 Livermore Trail
Killingworth, CT 06417

DISTRICT OF COLUMBIA
Botanical Society of Washington
Department of Biology — NHB/166
Smithsonian Institution
Washington, DC 20560

FLORIDA
Florida Native Plant Society
1203 Orange Avene
Winter Park, FL 32789

Florida Native Plant Society Chapters:
Big Pine Key
Central Florida
Coccoloba (N. Fort Myers)
Dade
Heartland (Hardee, Polk, Highland
Counties)
Magnolia (Tallahassee)
Martin County
Naples
Palm Beach
South Brevard
Suncoast (Tampa Bay)

Pensacola Wildflower Society
c/o Jim Dyehouse
3911 Dunwoody Drive
Pensacola, FL 32503

GEORGIA
Georgia Botanical Society
c/o Dr. Frank McCamey, Treasurer

1676 Andover Court
Doraville, GA 30360

HAWAII
Hawaiian Botanical Society
c/o Department of Botany
University of Hawaii
3190 Maile Way
Honolulu, HI 96822

IDAHO
Idaho Native Plant Society
USDA — Forest Service
Intermountain Forest and Range Experiment Station
316 East Myrtle Street
Boise, ID 83706

ILLINOIS
Illinois Native Plant Society
Department of Botany
Southern Illinois University
Carbondale, IL 62901

INDIANA
Assoc. for the Use of Native Vegetation in
Landscape through Education
(A.N.V.I.L.)
871 Shawnee Avenue
Lafayette, IN 47905

KANSAS
Kansas Wildflower Society
Mulvane Art Center
Washburn University
17th & Jewell Street
Topeka, KS 66621

Grassland Heritage Foundation
5450 Buena Vista
Shawnee Mission, KS 66205
(To encourage the preservation of native prairie and the use of native vegetation in the landscape).

Save the Tallgrass Prairie, Inc.
4101 West 54th Terrace
Shawnee Mission, KS 66025
(To protect a portion of the tallgrass prairie within the National Parks.)

LOUISIANA
Louisiana Native Plant Society
c/o Richard Johnson

Route 1, Box 151
Saline, LA 71070

Louisiana Native Plant Society Chapters:
Acadian
Alexandria
Natchitoches
Ruston

Greater New Orleans Native Plant Society
Mr. David Heikamp
717 Guiffias Avenue
Metairie, LA 70001

Northwest Louisiana Native Plant Society
Mrs. Karlene Defatta
Route 2, Box 54-C
Keithville, LA 71047

MAINE
Josselyn Botanical Society
c/o Dr. Charles D. Richards, President
Deering Hall
University of Maine
Orono, ME 04469

MARYLAND
Chesapeake Audubon Society
Rare Plant Committee
P.O. Box 3173
Baltimore, MD 21228

Maryland Native Plant Society
c/o Scaffidi
14720 Claude Lane
Silver Spring, MD 20904

MASSACHUSETTS
New England Botanical Club
Botanical Museums Avenue
Oxford Street
Cambridge, MA 02138

New England Wild Flower Society, Inc.
Garden in the Woods
Hemenway Road
Framingham, MA 01701

MICHIGAN
Michigan Botanical Club
Matthaei Botanical Gardens
1800 Dixboro Road
Ann Arbor, MI 48105

MINNESOTA

Minnesota Native Plant Society
220 BioSci Center
University of Minnesota
1445 Gortner Avenue
St. Paul, MN 55108

MISSISSIPPI
Mississippi Native Plant Society
c/o Travis Salley, Secretary
202 N. Andrews Avenue
Cleveland, MS 38732

MISSOURI
Missouri Native Plant Society
Box 6612
Jefferson City, MO 65102-6612

NEVADA
Northern Nevada Native Plant Society
Box 8965
Reno, NV 89507

NEW JERSEY
New Jersey Native Plant Society
c/o Frelinghuysen Arboretum
Box 1295R
Morristown, NJ 07960

NEW MEXICO
Native Plant Society of New Mexico
P.O. Box 5917
Santa Fe, NM 87502

NEW YORK
Syracuse Botanical Club
Janet Holmes
306 Cleveland Boulevard
Fayetteville, NY 13066

Torrey Botanical Club
New York Botanical Garden
Bronx, NY 10458

NORTH CAROLINA
North Carolina Wildflower Preservation Society
c/o North Carolina Botanical Garden
UNC-CH Totten Center 457-A
Chapel Hill, NC 27514

Western Carolina Botanical Club
Richard M. Smith, President
Tinequa Drive
Connestee Falls

Brevard, NC 28712

OHIO
Cincinnati Wildflower Preservation Society
c/o Dr. Victor G. Soukup
Department of Biology
University of Cincinnati
Cincinnati, OH 45221

Ohio Native Plant Society
c/o Ann Malmquist, President
6 Louise Drive
Chagrin Falls, OH 44022

OREGON
Native Plant Society of Oregon
c/o Dr. Frank A. Lang
Department of Biology
Southern Oregon State College
Ashland, OR 97520

PENNSYLVANIA
Botanical Society of Pittsburgh
c/o Mr. Robert F. Bahl
401 Clearview Avenue
Pittsburgh, PA 15205

Muhlenberg Botanical Society
c/o North Museum
Franklin and Marshall College
Lancaster, PA 17604

Pennsylvania Native Plant Society
1806 Commonwealth Building
316 Fourth Avenue
Pittsburgh, PA 15222

Philadelphia Botanical Club
Academy of Natural Sciences
19th and the Parkway
Philadelphia, PA 19103

TENNESSEE
Tenneessee Native Plant Society
c/o Department of Botany
University of Tennessee
Knoxville, TN 37916

TEXAS
Big Thicket Association
Box 198
Saratoga, TX 77585
(To promote the preservation of the area of Southwest Texas known as the Big Thicket.)

Native Plant Society of Texas
P.O. Box 23836-TWU Station
Denton, TX 76204

UTAH
Utah Native Plant Society
c/o The State Arboretum of Utah
University of Utah, Building 436
Salt Lake City, UT 84112

VIRGINIA
Virginia Native Plant Society
P.O. Box 844
Annandale, VA 22003

Virginia Wildflower Preservation Society Chapters:
Blue Ridge, Roanoke
Jefferson, Charlottesville
John Clayton, Williamsburg
Piedmont, Warrenton
Pocahontas, Richmond
Potowmack, McLean
Prince William, Manassas
Shenandoah, Harrisonburg

WASHINGTON
Washington Native Plant Society
c/o Dr. Arthur R. Kruckeberg
Department of Botany
University of Washington
Seattle, WA 98195

Abundant Life Seed Foundation
Box 772, 1029 Lawrence
Gardiner, WA 98334
(To propagate and preserve native plants of the North Pacific Coast with emphasis on rare and endangered species.)

WEST VIRGINIA
West Virginia Native Plant Society
Herbarium, Brooks Hall
West Virginia University
Morgantown, WV 26506

WYOMING
Wyoming Native Plant Society
P.O. Box 1471 (a)nt Society
P.O. Box 1471
Cheyenne, WY 82001